Godly
Servants

Discipleship and Spiritual Formation
for Missionaries

David Teague

Mission
Imprints

For further resources and ordering information visit
www.godlyservants.org

GODLY SERVANTS: Discipleship and Spiritual Formation for Missionaries
Copyright © 2012 David P. Teague
All rights reserved.

ISBN-10: 0615607810
ISBN-13: 978-0615607818

Contents

Introduction

The purpose of this book is to help evangelical mission workers to intentionally deepen their Christian spirituality. There are now a multitude of books available on discipleship and spiritual formation, but very little has been written specifically for missionaries. Mission work presents its own unique challenges that require a specialized treatment.

This material was originally developed within the context of Interserve, an interdenominational and evangelical organization of over 800 workers who serve in more than 30 countries. As one of its organizational goals, Interserve wished to deepen its spirituality. As part of that initiative, I was asked to form a team which then presented "Godly Leadership" seminars to over 70 leaders. This book is an outgrowth of those seminars and all the valuable feedback we received from our participants.

I wish to thank those who were our main team partners: Winnie Thuma, Karen Tan, Dr. Harvey Shepard and Ellen Alexander. Also involved were Maggie Le-Roy, Annieke van Dijk and Anne de Reybekill. I also convey special thanks to the initial help given by Dr. Paul Bender-Samuel, David Allen, Dr. Liu Ming and Doug Stewart, among many others.

Dr. David P. Teague

Part One: Communion

1
Intentional Spiritual Growth

Perhaps you have picked up this book because you want to prepare yourself for future mission service. Perhaps you already are a missionary but feel spiritually dry and depleted. Or, it may be that you are someone who is seeking a spiritual anointing and empowerment from God. Whatever may be your reason for reading this book, our prayer is that it may help you to be spiritually strengthened.

A high correlation has been observed between having a strong spiritual life and being effective and able to endure as a missionary. It is not enough just to pray occasionally and attend worship weekly. We need a more systematic understanding and approach to our own spiritual growth. We need to practice intentional spiritual formation.

In this first chapter, we will lay a foundation so that you can understand the basics of spiritual formation. In the later chapters, we will go into more depth and application.

What is Spiritual Formation?

Christian spiritual formation refers to the development of the image of Christ within us. Different authors have slightly different definitions, but all their descriptions tend to converge around this idea of our personal transformation into the image of Christ.

This transformation happens by our growth in three areas of our lives: (1) our personal relationship with God, (2) our relationship with others in Christian community, and (3) our involvement in

God's mission. Another way of saying this is, growth needs to take place in: "Communion, Community and Ministry."

Henri Nouwen (1932-1996), first spoke of this triad and it has now become a recurring theme in spiritual formation literature. The three main sections of this book are also based on it. We cannot grow spiritually just by seeking God alone. We also need to learn to love and serve others in the body of Christ and to do God's work in this world.

The result leads to a total transformation of our lives — involving our "head, heart and hands." Spiritual formation affects not just our thinking, will and affections, but also our character, habits, lifestyle choices and personal relationships. The goal is to develop a desire for God that affects every aspect of who we are and what we do. Spiritual formation is spiritual growth.

All of this leads to the following definition:

Spiritual Formation
Spiritual formation is the development of the image of Christ within us as we grow to know God, to love and serve other believers and to do God's mission in the world.

Is Spiritual Formation Biblical?

The phrase "spiritual formation" does not occur in the Bible, but the concept is certainly present. Four verses specifically include the word "formation" in some way when talking about spiritual growth:

Romans 8:29 For those God foreknew he also predestined to be <u>conformed</u> to the image of his Son, that he might be the firstborn among many brothers and sisters. (2011 NIV, as in all biblical quotes)

Romans 12:2 Do not conform to the pattern of this world, but be <u>transformed</u> by the renewing of your mind. Then you will be able to *test and approve what God's will is—his good, pleasing and perfect will.*

2 Corinthians 12:2 *And we all, who with unveiled faces contemplate the Lord's glory, are being <u>transformed</u> into his image with ever-increasing glory, which comes from the Lord, who is the Spirit.*

Galatians 4:19 *My dear children, for whom I am again in the pains of childbirth until Christ is <u>formed</u> in you …*

The underlined words in the verses above (*conformed, transformed* and *formed*) are all based on the Greek word *morphē*, which has to do with formation.

In addition, there are also other major verses which speak of spiritual growth through inner transformation, such as:

Ephesians 4:11-13 *So Christ himself gave the apostles, the prophets, the evangelists, the pastors and teachers, to equip his people for works of service, so that the body of Christ may be built up until we all reach unity in the faith and in the knowledge of the Son of God and become mature, attaining to the whole measure of the fullness of Christ.*

Ephesians 4:22-24 *You were taught, with regard to your former way of life, to put off your old self, which is being corrupted by its deceitful desires; to be made new in the attitude of your minds; and to put on the new self, created to be like God in true righteousness and holiness.*

Colossians 3:10 *… put on the new self, which is being renewed in knowledge in the image of its Creator.*

1 John 3:2 *Dear friends, now we are children of God, and what we will be has not yet been made known. But we know that when Christ appears, we shall be like him, for we shall see him as he is.*

These verses are frequently quoted in spiritual formation writings. They suggest that spiritual formation is really no different than spiritual growth — it's our progress in sanctification.

If this is so, then why do some evangelicals consider spiritual formation to be unbiblical? There are three chief reasons.

First, the word *spiritual* can mean different things to different people. For some unbelievers, spirituality refers to the "Good, the True and the Beautiful" rather than to the action of the Holy Spirit in their lives. For these people, spiritual formation would mean something like a walk in a park instead of growing into the image of Christ.

Secondly, some non-evangelicals who write about spiritual formation mistakenly confuse Christian mediation with the mind-emptying techniques of Buddhism. True Christian meditation is never mind-emptying, but rather is a means to becoming more mindful of God.

Thirdly, some evangelicals react against the phrase "spiritual formation" because it is relatively new to us — being largely a carry-over from Roman Catholic spiritual writers.

If there are problems with the phrase *spiritual formation*, then why should we even use it? Why not just continue with the older words, *disciple* and *discipleship*, which evangelicals already know and love? And what is the difference between spiritual formation and discipleship anyways?

Spiritual Formation and Discipleship Compared

The difference between spiritual formation and discipleship is one of emphasis. The word *discipleship* emphasizes our obedience to Christ, while the phrase *spiritual formation* emphasizes our internal transformation which enables obedience.

We see this in the New Testament itself. There, the word "disciple" (*mathētēs*) occurs 261 times — all of which are in the

Gospels and Acts because the word is closely associated with Christ. The original disciples followed Jesus physically. He taught them daily and gave them commands to follow.

In contrast, Paul never once uses the word "disciple." Indeed, when he wrote, Jesus was no longer personally discipling his followers. Instead, the Holy Spirit was doing the teaching and guiding. This is why Paul writes extensively about our interior spiritual transformation which enables obedience — a theme which the Gospels never really develops.

Sometimes we focus on the obedience part and forget about the transformation part. We know what to do, but we find it hard to do it. We know that we should be more loving, more forgiving and more caring, but then we get frustrated because our hearts do not cooperate. We need to remind ourselves that spiritual growth is a gradual process of maturation, not just following commands.

Over the centuries, two different bodies of spiritual writings have grown up around these two emphases of obedience and transformation. *Discipleship writings* focus on our obedience to Jesus' commands. Evangelical Protestants are very familiar with these writings. On the other hand, *spiritual formation writings* try to understand how the Spirit changes us within. Evangelicals are less familiar with these writings, but we have become more so since 1980. Both traditions of writings are important.

Effort and Grace

Some evangelicals feel that any disciplined effort on our part to grow spiritually is "human strength" that replaces God's grace. We're afraid that disciplines easily turn into obligations which can then degenerate into legalisms. We want to be inspired, not just to be dutiful!

Generally speaking, this tendency within evangelicalism has discouraged us from developing a spirituality that is intentional and methodical. True, there have been notable exceptions in history. John Wesley taught his followers to be very methodical — which is why they were called Methodists — but his example tends to be the exception rather than the rule among evangelicals.

It would help for us to have a more precise understanding of the relationship between effort and grace. There have been three approaches:

1. *Spiritual formation depends entirely on what we do.*

2. *Spiritual formation depends entirely on what God does.*

3. *Spiritual formation depends on what we do with God.*

The biblical evidence seems to favor the third choice, namely that spiritual growth is a cooperative effort between God and us. As Paul said:

Philippians 2:12-13 ... *continue to work out your salvation with fear and trembling, for it is God who works in you to will and to act in order to fulfill his good purpose.*

This explains why Scripture uses strenuous images to describe the spiritual life. We are on a journey, a pilgrimage, a narrow path and "The Way." In this world, we are exiles seeking a better place. Like the tribe of Israel, we are wandering through a desert. We are exhorted to endure persecution and suffering. Paul reminds us that we are soldiers who must withstand onslaughts (Ephesians 6:10-18). We are God's athletes who must go "into strict training" (1 Corinthians 9:25).

2 Peter also emphasizes the place of effort in spiritual formation:

2 Peter 1:5-8 *For this very reason, make every effort to add to your faith goodness; and to goodness, knowledge; and to knowledge, self-control; and to self-control, perseverance; and to perseverance, godliness; and to godliness, mutual affection; and to mutual affection, love. For if you possess these qualities in increasing* *measure, they will keep you from being ineffective and unproductive in your knowledge of our Lord Jesus Christ.*

Judging from these verses, grace and effort are complements rather than opposites. Effort enhances grace and grace empowers effort. That means when we do things out of a sense of duty or obligation, God can still work his grace through our efforts.

It is simplistic to think of grace as the opposite of effort. Many cultures make little distinction between love and duty. If your parents are in need, your loving duty is to care for them even if it is difficult. When we make an effort to fulfill a duty, affective feelings often follow over time. It is the same way when we make an effort to serve God by fulfilling necessary duties which may be difficult. Grace can work through all our hard work and efforts.

Can effort, then, ever be wrong? Dallas Willard informs us that it can in his advice: "God is not opposed to effort but to *earning*." That's the important distinction. Effort is complementary with grace so long as we are not trying to win favor from God.

Is it proper, then, to approach our own spiritual formation in an intentional and even methodical way? The answer is a resounding "Yes" since taking responsibility for our own spiritual growth is entirely consistent with living in grace. Spiritual maturity comes to those who are spiritually responsible for themselves.

Living Under Grace

Having argued for the place of effort in our spiritual lives, we must also reaffirm the role of grace.

Grace is unmerited favor. In many cultures, grace is a difficult concept to grasp since people are expected to return any favors done for them. There's a saying in Mandarin Chinese that goes: "If you give me a drop of water, I'll give you a fountain." It speaks of the expectation of reciprocity. When we feel that a kindness must always be reciprocated, it keeps us from understanding grace. God has to teach us what grace means.

A God of Grace

The first time that God describes his character in any detail is in Exodus 34 and there he emphasizes his gracious nature. God is a constant giver by nature who can never be repaid:

> *Exodus 34:6-7 The LORD, the LORD, the compassionate and gracious God, slow to anger, abounding in love and faithfulness, maintaining love to thousands, and forgiving wickedness, rebellion and sin. Yet he does not leave the guilty unpunished; he punishes the children and their children for the sin of the parents to the third and fourth generation.*

In Scripture, grace is the normal way by which God relates to his people. Just think of all the stories of God's unmerited favor shown to Israel such as the Exodus, the return from exile and the coming of Christ. God even shows grace to those who are evil: "He causes his sun to rise on the evil and the good, and sends rain on the righteous and the unrighteous" (Matthew 5:45).

For the Christian, *grace is the unmerited favor by which God saves us,* but grace pertains to much more than our initial salvation. *It is also the unmerited power by which God helps us to live for him.* In fact, the vast majority of the references to grace in the New Testament are not about our initial salvation, but God's continuing help for us.

If we are meant to live under God's grace every day, how can we learn do so? Here are a few suggestions.

Learning to Live under God's Grace

1. *Become truly convinced that God is a God of grace.* If you were to write a description of God's character, how prominent would *graciousness* be? Or do you think of God as mostly demanding?

2. *Learn to receive from God.* God is at work constantly all around us. Do we see it? Do we respond to it? Are we sensitive to the promptings of the Holy Spirit? Do we really regard God as a constant giver to us as we walk through our days?

3. *Let gratitude be your primary motive for serving God.* Even though we have to do many things out of duty, we must always remember to be grateful that we can even serve.

4. *Use your grace-gifts.* God distributes among us *charismata*, gifts of grace, through which God works his power for the edification of others (Ephesians 4:7-16). It's a joy to use them.

5. *Create a community of grace.* When we give away God's grace to each other, we create a community of grace. We do this by loving, forgiving, being generous, thoughtful and expecting nothing in return.

6. *Shape your self-identity around grace.* Is your identity shaped mostly by what you do for God, or by what God has done and is doing for you?

7. *Be humble in your walk before God.* Pride limits the workings of God's grace in our lives, as the story of the "Pharisee and the Tax Collector" tells us from Luke 18.

8. *Understand that God accepts us even though we are imperfect.* We are "Christians under Construction." Since there is no condemnation in Christ (Romans 8:1), we need to learn to give grace to ourselves when we are imperfect.

Grace and Revivals

There will be days when our walk with God will seem like a hard slog through the mud and rain. But there will also come moments of grace when God breaks through like the sun shining from behind clouds. Call it "inspiration" or "anointing" or "revival blessing" — God can suddenly inject grace into our weary hearts and help us function on a higher plane. Grace is not just the unmerited favor by which God saves us. It is also the unmerited power by which God helps us to live for him.

A spiritual awakening is an intensified work of the Holy Spirit that convicts, converts and consecrates us. In it, we gain a fresh vision of God and become more aware of God's nearness, holiness and majesty.

When we do our mission work, we must not only depend on our regular spiritual disciplines but we also need to call out to God to send us special times of spiritual blessing, anointing and grace. We certainly should make an intentional effort to grow spiritually, yet we also know that we need the anointing of grace.

A Balanced Spirituality

In thinking about Christian spirituality, then, it is very important that we maintain our balance. It is so easy for us to begin emphasizing one thing over another.

For instance, we might focus too much on effort and forget about anointing. Or, we might concentrate too much on the role of the Holy Spirit and neglect the study of Scripture. We might become legalistic —which is an attempt to earn God's favor. Or we might become antinomian — which happens when we value our individual freedom above the law of Christ. And we never forget to keep our faith centered on the atoning death and resurrection of our Savior, Jesus.

A balanced spiritual life, then, would look like this:

- *Based on Grace*

- *Strengthened by Effort*

- *Informed by Scripture*

- *Enabled by the Spirit*

- *Centered on Christ*

This is our touchstone by which we can test the quality of our spiritual formation. When we keep these five essential elements in mind, we have a guide to make needed corrections in our lives.

Spiritual Formation as a Progression

For centuries, writers have pictured spiritual formation as a progression in which we journey through three stages.

The first stage they called *purgation*. It is when we initially repent of every known sin in our lives once we come to Christ. The second stage is *illumination*. This is when God enlightens our hearts as we meditate in the Bible and pray. The third stage is *union*, when God infuses grace into our lives and transforms us to be like Christ.

In medieval times, writers took this idea of progression and developed it into very detailed schemes. For instance, in her book, the *Interior Castle*, St. Teresa of Avila says there are seven stages of increasingly higher grades of perfection. She likens the soul as going through these stages, which she winsomely depicts as rooms where we encounter Christ more and more.

For centuries, the idea of progression provided the blueprint for spiritual formation. It was a helpful way by which people imagined spiritual growth to be, but it also leads to some major problems

First, it tends to create a spiritual hierarchy in the church between "novices" and "saints." The spiritual contributions of beginners tends to be minimized in favor of those considered to be more spiritually advanced. Even to this day, the Roman Catholic Church calls priests, nuns and monks the "religious" while congregants are known as the "laity."

Secondly, it tends to impose a single path of spiritual formation onto everyone. For instance, St. Teresa's system relies heavily on contemplative prayer to promote spiritual growth, even though contemplation is a form of prayer which introverts find far easier to do than extroverts. Does this imply that only introverts can become "saints?"

Thirdly, it shifts the focus in salvation away from justification and places it almost exclusively on sanctification — which is a harmful imbalance, as will be explained.

Spiritual Formation as a Maturation

Although there is some merit in thinking of spiritual formation as a progression, Scripture describes it more simple as a maturation. Paul talks about the "worldly" and the "mere infants in Christ" (1 Corinthians 3:1) who are to become mature. Jesus' disciples matured into disciplers. He calls us "branches" which must mature until we can "bear fruit" (John 15).

In Scripture, the spiritual life consists of three great works of God within our lives: justification, sanctification and glorification. These steps are progressive in the sense that we begin at the Cross and end up in Glory, but they are not like progressively harder courses in a university. Rather, they are more like grand themes in which we gradually mature in our understanding. Spiritual formation is a process of working through the implications of justification, sanctification and glorification, more and more. All three are happening at the same time.

Justification

Justification indicates our legal standing with God. When we are justified before God, we are no longer under God's legal edict, his "wrath" — but we have been legally accepted by God because of the atoning work of Christ. This tells us to whom we belong. Because God has legally adopted us, we are now a part of his family. The change in our status is permanent and can never be denied.

This has several important implications in our lives as missionaries.

Often, missionaries are performance-driven people. We frequently feel that the only way we can please God is by working hard. This is not referring to the heartfelt desire to hear Jesus say, "Well done, good and faithful servant." Rather, it is the obsessive desire which makes us never relax — producing in us a constant sense of inadequacy and cheerlessness. Unchecked, it can lead to burn-out. *The doctrine of justification works against this obsession by reminding us that God is our heavenly Father.* Our sense of satisfaction is based ultimately on our relationship with our Father, not on our work. This comforts us, especially when disappointments affect our work.

Disappointments will happen. I spent five years on a Bible publishing project that failed because the publisher went bankrupt. Our friend, Eleanor Vandevort, spent years translating parts of the Bible into Nuer, a Sudanese language — only to have her work destroyed. Historically, John Eliot (c. 1604-1690), the first major Protestant missionary, saw most of his work among the Algonquin Indians come to an end during a colonial war. His own countrymen caused the death of many of his flock. We need to learn to find contentment in God alone, and not in our work or in our accomplishments.

The doctrine of justification also gives us a sense of identity. As missionaries, we often live with a confusion of identities as we encounter different cultures. We need a deep foundation within us to steady our lives.

I remember when our children asked me, "Daddy, who are we?" They were genuinely confused! Then, one day we took them to a 4th of July celebration at the American Embassy in Egypt. The place was packed with hotdogs, band music and lots of flags. Suddenly, my oldest daughter turned to me and said, "Now I know who we are. We're Americans!"

In a similar way, as missionaries, we need to gently remind ourselves and our families that we belong to God and we live under his providential care. As one older missionary once told me: "Begin each day with thinking just how much God loves you. Dwell on God's love over and over. Let it be the theme that you live by. You are loved. You belong to him." When we are secure in our relationship with God, we learn to forgive and be forgiven. We develop an identity filled with faith, grace, honesty, love and security in God.

Sanctification

Sanctification refers to the requirements we have for living in God's family. Since we belong to God and we live in God's home, we must live by God's rules and learn to please our heavenly Father. Missionary parents understand this, but our children might not.

Many missionary children appear to confuse sanctification with justification and this makes them often struggle with finding their own faith in Christ. From their earliest years, we have taught our children the requirements of being a Christian. We have raised them in our Christianized homes which have been heavily focused on the works of sanctification. Our children learn to say their prayers, go to church and do holy things, but they may do these things to please us rather than God.

They are very aware of the cost of discipleship because they have watched us work hard for Christ. Some children may feel like they can never live up to our level of discipleship. Although it was never our intent to discourage our children, just our lifestyle might make the Christian life appear too daunting and difficult for them.

By confusing sanctification with justification, mission children may also struggle with finding personal assurance of salvation even when they do believe in Christ. They may not feel that God loves them personally like we might feel. We can help them by reassuring them that they really are Christians once they believe that Jesus is the Lord and that God raised him from the dead (Romans 10:9). We can also tell them that the personal assurance of salvation — which is the Holy Spirit's inward testimony that we belong to God — eventually comes to us in God's own time as we live for God. It helps for children to follow age-appropriate spiritual disciplines.

Most missionary children know that the faith has requirements. What they especially need to do is to own the faith for themselves. If everything seems like a duty to them, they must learn the "first love" side of faith. It is proper for us as parents to teach our children the requirements of the faith, but we must also pray for our children to develop an affective love for God.

Glorification

Glorification concerns our family inheritance. God is rich! As members of his family, we have a share in those riches right now. Our eternal life has already begun.

The guarantee of our eternal riches is the Holy Spirit. Ephesians 1:13-14 describes the Spirit as being a "deposit" of all that is to come. This means, every time we experience the Holy Spirit in our lives — by convicting us, strengthening us, helping us resist temptation or gradually transforming us — it reminds us that we possess eternal life with God, which is already breaking into our lives right now. Glorification is the doctrine of eternity.

This teaching is important in mission work because it gives us hope, despite whatever happens.

I remember once when our mission team felt totally exhausted and discouraged. All we could see were the problems. There were setbacks, difficulties and sicknesses. Then, one of our team gave us a devotional talk about glory. He said, "Usually, we just see the problems and we can't see the glory we are achieving. The glory-side is there, but it usually is hidden. We either can focus on the problems, and let them overwhelm us, or we can catch glimpses of the glory and regain our perspective."

Sometimes we pray anxiously, hoping our problems will go away. At other times, it is better to just forget oneself in God's praise. A healthy spirituality knows when to say, "enough with it all," and just spend time enjoying God's sovereignty and grandeur. It is only when we are aware that glorification is not something that will happen in the future, but it is something that we are meant to experience right now as well, that we can put our problems in their proper place.

A Model of Spiritual Formation for Missions

Spiritual formation is a gradual process of maturation. It should never become a contest over who is more advanced. We are not in school competing for grades against each other. We are just brothers and sisters all living together in God's family. There is no hierarchy.

A wise person once told me, "We don't practice hierarchical discipling in our fellowship because we all have weaknesses, even those who are more mature in the faith." He then went on to explain, "In our fellowship, we don't designate a chosen few people to be the disciplers. Rather, we're all disciples together. We all support each other as we mature together. In the Bible, Christ discipled people, but none of us is Christ. Today, Christ is the body of Christ, the whole church."

That's a good model for how spiritual formation can be done in a mission organization. Spiritual formation should be a gradual, non-hierarchical, supportive process of maturation in which everyone's gifts are respected.

The Soul of a Servant

O nce I was the pastor of a church, founded in 1679, that had a fascinating mission history. It sent out some of the very first mission workers to Hawaii, particularly two women named Clarissa Chapman and Sybil Moseley.

Clarissa's Bible teaching caused a large revival to break out in Honolulu in the 1840's. People loved her and her husband, Richard. People also loved Sybil, but not *her* husband. Sybil was married to a very difficult man, Hiram Bingham.

Although Hiram was the initial leader of the mission, he was such a cantankerous man that when he and Sybil were on home leave, his fellow mission workers begged for him not to return. "Please keep Hiram away!" they asked.

Perhaps you have met a few mission workers with a personality like Hiram's. Our strong personalities may help us to endure, but they can also get in the way. Even Barnabas finally parted ways with his strong-willed mission partner, Paul.

It is common knowledge that many mission workers return prematurely to their home countries because of poor relationships with their colleagues. Some statistics have suggested this to be the *primary* reason for premature returns.

All of us — and not just the Hirams in our midst —suffer from personality defects. We're often very good at concealing these deficiencies when we need to, and especially from our supporters. But inwardly, we may often feel irritable, stretched, tired and quite human.

When mission organizations purposefully promote intentional spiritual formation within the ranks, however, it can change things. I am familiar with one mission that has been conducting a running experiment of intentional spiritual formation for over 30 years. I asked one of their leaders what the results have been. "It has brought deeper commitment, greater effectiveness and greater retention among our missionaries," was the reply.

Servants with Healthy Hearts

Consider three leaders from Scripture: Saul, his son Jonathan, and David:

SAUL was distrustful, full of envy and controlled by pride. His decisions lacked basic integrity.

JONATHAN was a wise leader. His actions promoted trust and good relationships. His leadership inspired confidence.

DAVID was a man of integrity who trusted in God instead of taking revenge. He was able to admit his faults.

All three said they were God's servants, yet Saul could hardly be called *godly.* Although God had called him, anointed him and even caused him to prophesy, Saul lacked authenticity with God. His human frailties affected him too much.

This leads us to ask, "How healthy is my heart? Although I may be serving God, am I truly healthy on the inside?"

We need to ask this question because spiritual formation happens in the heart, not the head. Although we may be well-trained and might even have attended seminary, each of us still needs to have a healthy heart.

Paul once prayed for the spiritual growth of his friends using a wonderful prayer, whose beauty I have tried to capture in the following original translation:

Ephesians 3:16-19
I pray that God's beautiful richness will make you strong.
May you experience the power of his Spirit deep down inside.
May Christ live in your hearts as you believe in him.
Rooted and grounded in love,
may you and all God's people understand Christ's love.
May you sense its width and length and height and depth.
May you know his love which is beyond knowing.
Then you will be filled with everything God has for you.

As this scripture explains, spiritual growth happens when Christ changes us gradually "deep down inside." Also, it does not happen merely by following rules but by experiencing God within a family of faith. Together, as we share the "beautiful richness" of God, the Spirit works and we become "filled with the fullness of God."

Godliness is not trying to be perfect. It is growing in grace. This happens only when we are honest about ourselves to God. This is why the Bible never air-brushes its main characters. We see Abraham, afraid and distrustful. We watch both Moses and David commit open murders. David cannot keep his pants on. Peter is a midnight traitor. Scripture colors them in all their faults, because the Story is not about perfection. It is about God's grace.

We simply do not grow spiritually when we are trying to be perfect. True spiritual growth only happens when we struggle with the darkest aspects of our personalities. "It is not the healthy who need a doctor but the sick," Jesus told us (Luke 5:31). The brokenness of our lives is the growing edge of our faith.

Our Irrational Side

For too long we have bought into the notion that our minds hold perfect control over our hearts. We have thought that spiritual growth happens simply by studying biblical principles. Yet, even the Bible tells us to do what the word says and not simply to listen to it. Informing the mind is the easy part. Changing one's life is a lot harder. Acquiring information alone does not lead to transformation. We have to integrate the information into our lives. This takes time and effort.

Scripture teaches us to be compassionate, yet it took me five years of chaplaincy work — dealing with the dying and daily medical dramas — to become more compassionate. The change did not happen just by reading about compassion. The change happened by facing several thousand people in crisis. Similarly, we will not grow spiritually just by reading this book. We will grow spiritually only as we struggle with the deep things within our lives and experience a gradual transformation there with the help of God.

We have to understand that none of us is completely rational. We're not logical machines who can will ourselves into godliness by just deciding in our minds to do so. We're people. And as people, we have all kinds of inbuilt flaws and mistakes. It's hard to rewire the heart.

The Apostle Paul acknowledged his own irrational side in words that recall a dog chasing its own tail:

Romans 7:15, 19   *"I do not understand what I do. For what I want to do I do not do, but what I hate I do ... What I do is not the good I want to do; no, the evil I do not want to do – this I keep on doing."*

We are more irrational than we may realize. In one famous experiment in the 1970's, Dr. Benjamin Libet found that our brains signal us to perform an action a fraction of a second *before* we consciously "choose" to do the action. This suggests that the irrational, subconscious part of our minds controls us far more than we recognize.

Since the time of the psychiatrist Carl Jung (1875-1961), some have called our irrational side the *shadow side*. The label is meant to describe all the suppressed emotions, unresolved fears, urges and conflicts that linger within our psyches that exert an irrational influence on our behavior.

The shadow side is the repository for our human brokenness. There collects all our sorrows and unsettled pain from the traumas of life we have experienced — including our unresolved grief, failures and abandonments. The shadow side partners with what the Bible calls our sinful nature to influence us.

A great deal of human behavior arises from our irrational instincts, impulses, habits, reactions and raw emotions. It has even been said that only 5% (if that much!) of human behavior is purely rational and planned. This is true even for Christians who were, on last check, still human.

Our irrational side can cause us to:
- Become addicted to pornography
- Save face at any cost
- Turn into a workaholic
- Gossip about others to gain power over them
- Become controlling
- Think that we are superior to others
- Be unable to form deep, lasting relationships
- Feel distrustful or always anxious
- Be too sensitive to criticism
- Be unable to walk away from harmful situations

Human brokenness also affects how we treat each other:
- We don't discuss issues openly or freely
- We communicate through third-parties
- We accept conflict as normal
- We lack empathy
- We don't feel safe around each other
- We practice conditional love and make inconsistent rules
- We fail to respect boundaries
- We remain inflexible
- We always expect perfection

Sometimes our shadow side leads us into truly self-destructive habits and behaviors. It's like the moray eel that lurks in an ocean crevice — all may seem calm and serene until the moment when the eel suddenly lunges and strikes. We may think we are completely in control until the day comes when we find ourselves doing stupid, self-destructive things. Just this last week, I spoke to a Christian man who had begun to binge drink because he is chronically unemployed and depressed. In his hopelessness, his irrational side is beginning to engulf him.

I also once knew a brilliant thoracic surgeon who treated the cancer victims of smoking. He smoked himself to death — dying of the same, painful disease he sought to cure in others. At his funeral, his best friend from their medical school days spoke of this man's incredible mind. But then he said incredulously, "Why did he do it? Why did he smoke? He knew better. It was so irrational."

We may think that we can control our irrational side through brute force, but what we really need is healing, not repression. In fact, psychological researchers have found a high correlation between a repressive religious upbringing and sex offenses. This does not mean that people from caring, Christian homes are going to turn into dangerous sex criminals. What it does imply is that a reliance on repressive rules alone, no matter how strictly enforced, is inadequate in suppressing the shadow side.

Missionaries and Our Shadows

Even missionaries cast a shadow. Although we may not be aware of our own shadow side, others will be. In the Bible, Paul seemed oblivious to his own obtuseness in his conflict with John Mark, but Barnabas was not. Similarly, we seem unable to perceive our deep faults like others can. A few of the more common human frailties among missionaries are narcissism, compulsive working, and a distorted sense of self-identity.

Narcissism

Some of us wonderful missionaries have a narcissistic tendency! That is, we always have to make ourselves look good. Everything always has to revolve around us!

Narcissism is especially common among leaders. In a survey of more than 1,200 employees, Wayne Hochwarter, a management professor, found that 31% percent reported having a narcissistic boss who exaggerated his or her accomplishments. Hochwarter also found that these leaders created a toxic environment around whom "the team perspective ceases to exist, and the work environment becomes increasingly stressful." Often, such leaders are unaware of how others perceive them.[1]

I knew a physician with a narcissistic tendency. He was aware of this propensity within himself, but found it difficult to overcome. As a child, he had been abandoned and this created an insecurity that drove him to earn the love of others. It was the reason why he rendered extraordinary service as a physician —to win acceptance and praise. He often made himself to be so much the center of attention that it weakened his ability to be a team player.

When we are inclined toward narcissism, it is very important to bathe ourselves in the unconditional love of our heavenly Father. Only God's love can fill the love hunger within us. Narcissists especially need to cultivate a solid understanding of justification and a devotional life that is immersed in God's love.

Compulsive Working

Sometimes, God's servants can be compulsive workaholics. When we're like this, we are performance-driven and live under the tyranny of the urgent. Our identities can become so intertwined with our work that we might be reluctant ever to go on a spiritual retreat. We begin adopting scripted roles instead of relating to others in real friendships. We can also forget how to rest and play.

Since the needs around us are so great, it is easy for us to justify working compulsively, but it's a serious spiritual problem. On some level, we have forgotten how to live under God's sovereignty. We do not trust God and feel the need to do everything. This is idolatry.

A good way to begin a different lifestyle is to practice Sabbath-keeping, the spiritual discipline which is designed to keep work from becoming idolatrous. Sabbath-keeping reminds us that God is ultimately the one who is in control.

When we are very young and others are taking care of us, we sense that all is well. This frees us from worry and we can play carefree. In the same way, as God's children, when we keep the Sabbath and rest, we are enjoying God's sovereign care. The Sabbath is meant to free us from worry so we can learn to play again.

A Distorted Self-identity

Another shadow that is common among missionaries is a distorted self-identity. This is especially true if we occupy an important professional role in a host country, or live on an economic scale that is higher than the people we serve. We might actually start thinking that we are innately more significant than others.

Sometimes, we feel like celebrities! Wherever we go, people always seem to treat us differently. Our church supporters often place us on pedestals while the people we serve might consider us elites. Some of us can be recognized anywhere in a large city or even in a whole country. I was genuinely worried that our young children were beginning to think they were royalty.

Power can also affect our self-identities in very subtle ways.

In one research study it was found that whenever we have power, we immediately begin judging others more strictly and ourselves more leniently. In other words, power tends to turn us into moral hypocrites. Our self-identity excuses us while causing us to hold others to a different standard.[2]

In a similar way, when we lose power, such as when we leave a high-profile position, it can take months to feel normal again. We are no longer the important professional. We're just back to being an "ordinary" disciple like anyone else. It can be easy to forget what it is like to just being a disciple without an important title.

From a spiritual standpoint, we can do several things to correct a distorted self-identity. Of course, we need to remind ourselves of our real identity: that God has adopted us and we belong to him. Besides this, we might also need to do something really radical to rebalance ourselves. For instance, after completing service in a position of power, we might voluntarily take on a position with less power. Instead of always being the important administrator, we might choose to go back to line work.

Healing Happens as we Develop Intimacy with God

As missionaries, we are like actors who play a role. People expect us to be wise, encouraging and visionary and, to the best of our abilities, we try to live up to these expectations.

In reality, though, the public personas we project on stage are quite different from our private lives. As missionaries, we may feel disconnected between what we do and who we really are. Alone, we might find ourselves feeling confused and discouraged, or struggling with self-doubt and resentment. The soul-numbing pressures and demands of our jobs can cause us to grow out-of-touch with ourselves.

Added to this is the inherent capacity at self-deception with which we are all born and which just gets worse when we get busy — a deception that deludes us into thinking that all is well, even while our souls are withering inside us.

Inner healing comes to us through developing intimacy with God. This is another foundational principle of spiritual formation.

The word "intimacy" in English sounds like the words "into-me-see." It reminds us of those tropical fish that are transparent. You can see all their little bones and intestines inside them. To be intimate with God, we have to be like those fish. We have to allow God to see inside of us. But we don't like being those little fish. We don't like having anyone see into us. We only allow ourselves to be vulnerable when we feel absolutely safe.

Zacchaeus in the tree could admit who he was only after he felt that Jesus loved him. It's the same with us. Until we feel that God loves us and cares for us, we will find it difficult to be honest about ourselves.

So, spiritual formation requires us to be honest with what is inside us, but we will not be honest until we feel safe and loved. That is how spiritual formation works. And that is why spiritual formation writers place so much emphasis on the love of God.

The heart of spiritual formation is not doing spiritual disciplines and going on perpetual retreats. Rather, it is to bathe our souls in the love of God. To grow spiritually, the secret is to dwell on the love of God — filling our hearts and minds with it each day!

Be truly convinced in your heart that God is good and safe and loving. Realize that he understands you like a father or a mother. He knows all our strengths and weaknesses yet still cares for us. You can talk to him freely about anything. When we know that God loves us, it frees us and we can begin to experience inner healing.

The Good Side to the Shadow Side

There is a good side to the shadow side. The deepest pain we feel often becomes the motivation that fuels our strongest drives. The point is not to deny our shadow side, but to have God redeem it so it can be used for his glory.

Our shadow side is intrinsic to us all. Just as we cannot outrun our own shadow on a sunny day, none of us can deny who we are. To do so would be to disown our own humanity. We are who we are, and God knows this. He understands our humanity and providentially shapes our personalities. God does not want us to be false to ourselves. Instead, he desires us to be honest about our humanity and to allow his grace to transform us into something more honoring to him. God's grace does not change our personalities as much as it sanctifies who we are.

3

Becoming Sensitive to God

Through the centuries, the chief question which spiritual teachers have asked those who came to them for spiritual counsel has been, "How is your prayer life?"

Our prayer lives indicate what is happening in our relationship with God. Has our prayer become dry? Does it seem stuck? Has it turned into mostly a routine or a duty?

This chapter is about the subject of becoming sensitive to God, but it is based on the idea that we grow closer to God as we grow in our prayer relationship with God.

What is Prayer?

It seems so simple to ask, "What is prayer?" – yet people have so many different answers. Secular people often see prayer as a form of self-talk: people addressing God but really just muttering to themselves. Others treat prayer like magic: people somehow releasing a mysterious power into the world by giving voice to their wishes.

Among Christians, two views dominate. Some treat prayer as an obligation or a duty to be fulfilled before God. And so, they "say their prayers." Many other Christians think of prayer as "talking with God." That's how we often teach our children and new believers about prayer. We say, "Just start talking to God!" But, while this understanding of prayer may be helpful, even it is limited since prayer is much more than just talking.

One of the oldest studies on prayer comes from Evagrious the Solitary (346-399 AD), one of the Desert Fathers. In his work, *On*

Prayer, he says that: "Prayer is communing with God in the depths of our hearts."

The phrase, "depths of our hearts" translates the Greek word **nous** (νους). Evagrious and the other Desert Fathers considered the *nous* to be our faculty for comprehending God. Some of the Desert Fathers even called the *nous,* the "organ of contemplation."

Evagrious realized something important: we encounter God only in our place of deepest honesty. The heart is the wellspring of life out of which flows our values, actions, emotions, intellect, habits and will. If we are honest to God there, we will also become sensitive to God.

Once we understand prayer as communing with God in the depths of our soul, it leads to three important implications about prayer:

1. Prayer is as Varied as the Ways We Relate to God

First, it first tells us that the form of our prayer depends on what is happening in our relationship with God at the moment. So, if we have sinned, our prayer will be repentance. If we are grateful, our prayer will be thanksgiving and praise. When we are in need, we petition God. When we are burdened for another person, we intercede. The prayer form depends on our relationship with God.

2. Prayer Can Be Non-Verbal

Secondly, prayer can be non-verbal since we can relate to God without words. When we think of prayer as simply "talking to God," we rarely explore the non-verbal aspects of prayer, such as is found in contemplative prayer.

3. God Can Also Take the Initiative

Thirdly, since prayer is communing with God, it must also be true that God can take the initiative in the relationship at times.

Imagine living near a farm that has cows and sells delicious ice cream. Sometimes you would say, "Let's go there and get some of that wonderful ice cream," but sometimes someone else would be sure to make the suggestion. In all good friendships, each one can be the initiator. And it is like that in our prayer relationship with God as well: sometimes God does the initiating.

And so, Luke 10:21 speaks of Jesus rejoicing "in the Spirit." And Romans 8:26 says, "We do not know what we ought to pray for, but the Spirit himself intercedes for us through wordless groans." Ephesians 6:18 mentions, "Pray in the Spirit on all occasions with all kinds of prayers and requests." And Jude 1:20 says, "praying in the Holy Spirit, keep yourselves in God's love." These verses speak about God's Spirit moving within us as we pray.

Perhaps you have experienced the movements of God within your heart during prayer: such as joys, burdens, groans, longings, promptings and urges. It may be a deep yearning to intercede for someone or a sense of hunger than can only be met through prayer. We learn the difference between true burdens from the Spirit and our own vain imaginations by growing in spiritual discernment. That comes through practicing humility and always being honest to God.

Evagrious' definition of prayer, with its three implications, helps us to become sensitive to God. Now, let's continue to work this out in more detail.

A Deep and Continuing Repentance

The most important step in becoming sensitive to God is to make a deep and continuing repentance. Unless we repent, sin will continue to deceive us and harden our hearts.

The Desert Fathers considered deep repentance to be essential to a healthy prayer life. They taught that the human heart is dull and callous toward God and filled with sinful desires and tendencies.

They considered these sinful desires— things like anger, envy, sloth, lust and pride, among other sins[1] — to be passions that control us and govern our behavior. They taught that whenever sinful passions control us, a demonic component also will be present. Their thinking is similar to Paul's in Ephesians 2:1-3, when he talked about the spirit which is now "at work in those who are disobedient," who live to gratify their "cravings." In such a state we cannot pray.

A deep and continuing repentance involves a careful review of our lives, turning from all known evil with heartfelt compunction, seeking forgiveness from God and reconciliation with others. Unfortunately, we tend to shorten this soul work in the modern era, even for our own lives. The Desert Fathers would not have understood any talk about "accepting Jesus" unless it also included a soulful reconciliation with God.

Repentance is difficult work, but totally necessary. It is like the butterfly which must struggle out of its own cocoon to become strong enough to live. Unless we wriggle out of ourselves through repentance, we will never be able to live for God. Deep repentance enables us to escape the cocoon of ourselves.

St. Augustine (354-430 AD) in his autobiography, known to us as the *Confessions*, taught the world how to live a life of deep and continuing repentance.

In one famous passage, he obsesses over the day he stole some pears as a boy. This hardly seems to be scintillating material for a tell-all confession, yet in his *Confessions* Augustine is telling us the story of his soul. On the day he took those pears, he lost his innocence. He was Adam in the Garden again, snitching God's forbidden fruit and deceiving himself in the grabbing. It was the first of many drubbings he gave his soul, leading into years of self-deception. That's why he dwelt on those pears, to undo the deception.

Augustine also writes of the day, years later, when he came to know God. He had become convinced of the Gospel by then, but could not free himself from his lusts. In agony, he went into a garden to wrestle with his soul. There, with tears flowing profusely down his face, Augustine hears a child in a neighboring house call out the words, *"Tolle, lege"* — "Pick it up! Read it!" Thinking it to be a sign from God, Augustine picks up the copy of Romans he has with him and his eyes randomly fall on the words from Romans 13:13-14:

Let us behave decently, as in the daytime, not in carousing and drunkenness, not in sexual immorality and debauchery, not in dissension and jealousy. Rather, clothe yourselves with the Lord Jesus Christ, and do not think about how to gratify the desires of the flesh.

"As the sentence ended," Augustine writes, "there was infused in my heart something like the light of full certainty and all the gloom of doubt vanished away.[2] He was free. Later, he was to write, "To hear from You about oneself is to know oneself."[3]

Only God's searing presence and enabling grace can show us what we really are and also free us at the same time. Repentance is otherwise impossible or always will be insincere. When we come to this moment of knowledge, it is often marked with tears and shame, but also with release and joy, as we realize that Christ really did die for us.

In the words of St. Isaiah the Solitary, one of the early desert fathers:

We do not see our sins unless we sever ourselves from them with a feeling of revulsion. Those who have reached this level pray to God with tears, and are filled with shame when they recall their evil love of the passions. [4]

The Psalmist versifies about unrepentant people who tearlessly "flatter themselves too much to detect or hate their sin" (Psalm 36:1-2). But when we encounter the living God, we know we cannot play at our games anymore. God is too much the keen detective. When he shines his light upon us, we can no longer hide behind our pride or deny our human brokenness; we can only admit who we are. By so doing, we come to know both God and ourselves.

The Makeover

God's purpose is our makeover, since salvation is wholeness — eternal and spiritual. The makeover of a human heart takes years since it is heart work, not just head work. We can memorize every verse in the Bible and read every book there is on spiritual formation and still not know what it all means. But when we do our heart work in a genuine way, the result is a growing trust in God's adequacy.

The makeover is a process of re-creation: God confronting our selfish and judging spirit, draining the acid out of our hate and converting our stubborn resentment into forgiveness. Spiritual transformation is God descending into the hidden depths of our underground mine, shining his light along the long-darkened path and chiseling out our self-deception.

We may, for instance, know that we belong to Christ yet still habitually lash out at people who criticize us. Then, one day the thought dawns on us, "If Christ is my righteousness, why am I so upset when people criticize me? What does it matter what others think about me? I am living for Christ now, not for myself." Realizing this, we relax. We ease ourselves into God's adequacy. It is the Spirit at work, transforming us, the makeover happening.

The ultimate goal of spiritual formation is always an increasing trust in God's sufficiency for our lives. Without God, we are like people who have to live out of a suitcase — with all the insecurities, fears and wants of being homeless. But when we live with God, we know we have a home. He provides us with security, reassurance and comfort — all the blessings which gradually change us as people.

A Continual Weeding

In the years I grew strawberries for my children, my patch produced buckets of spring-sweet berries. However, when I got busy and neglected the patch, it yielded arm-loads of weeds instead.

The human heart is very much like that. Unless we take care of it, the heart will always revert back to its native species — all the worries, infatuations and frenzies that so easily plague us. Affections for God are a cultivated fruit, like strawberries; they do not come naturally. We need to continually weed our hearts.

Confession is spiritual weeding. It is bending over, taking a close look at our lives and pulling out what needs to go. Confession is when we make our hearts true to God. Done right, confession is good for the soul. It is another way we learn to trust in God's sufficiency.

Again, Augustine teaches us. His book, the *Confessions*, was the world's first spiritual autobiography, an intensely personal writing with a consciousness of God's presence. No one had ever written anything like it, especially since they lived in an honor and shame culture in which no one would ever admit a fault.

Never mind, Augustine wrote freely about his faults. About his soul. About his soul struggling to know God. No one ever made themselves look so vulnerable like that on paper before — no one except Augustine. That's why his book proved to be so powerful, because it knifed through all the hypocrisy of the late Roman Empire. And that's why Augustine so singularly has taught the world what it means to live a life of confession. He writes in his *Confessions* (1.5):

> *The house of my soul is too small for you to come to it. Enlarge it. It is in ruins. Restore it. In your eyes, it looks offensive. I admit it. I know it. But who will clean it up? To whom shall I call other than you?*

His soul is talking, talking with God. All the time, talking. His soul is seeking, always seeking. Augustine is taking care of his garden. He is paying attention to the state of his heart. He is coming alive to God.

Spiritual formation writers have always stressed the need for self-examination. To be alive to God we must keep our relationship fresh by renouncing evil and remembering providence. Throughout history, different groups and people have developed various systems to do this. St. Ignatius of Loyola taught his disciples to review their lives daily with something he called *examen* prayer. Similarly, the English Puritans customarily kept diaries in which they examined their spiritual journeys. The exact format of our self-examination is not as important as the intent: that we do whatever we must to keep our hearts responsive to God.

Over time, what is in our hearts will affect the organizations we serve. Narrow-hearted missionaries surely create narrow-minded organizations. Great-hearted missionaries create open, flourishing organizations. Augustine took the time to cultivate his soul, which is why he was the most influential Christian in his day. As we cultivate our souls, we will influence our world as well. After all, Jesus taught that everything flows from within: "For out of the heart come evil thoughts — murder, adultery, sexual immorality, theft, false testimony, slander. These are what defile a person" (Matthew 15:19-20a). On the other hand, "The good person brings good things out of the good stored up within the heart" (Luke 6:45).

4
Going Deeper with God

H ebrews 3:13 warns us that we can become "hardened by sin's deceitfulness." That is, we can lose the ability to hear the voice of God in our hearts.

The opposite of this is also true. When we become alive and more sensitive to God, we are more able to hear God's voice. This is why, as we go deeper with God, we need to learn about something called listening prayer.

Listening Prayer

In 1 Kings 19, the prophet Elijah wanders deep into the desert. He had been involved in a series of dramatic power encounters with the followers of Baal, but now he is alone and discouraged. Elijah desperately needs renewal and direction.

Huddled in his mountain cave, Elijah watches as a parade of wind, earthquake and fire go by. His previous ministry had been a drama like that. Fire had fallen from the sky at Mount Carmel. And Elijah had run with supernatural strength through a blinding, wind-driven rain. As a prophet, he really had shaken up those followers of Baal.

Now, God is weaning him from all that. The parade over, Elijah encounters a "still, small voice." More precisely, the phrase in Hebrew is the "sound of utter silence." God was moving in quiet truth within Elijah's heart. There on the mountain, as Elijah heard God speak, his life was healed and his ministry redirected.

What happened to Elijah on that mountain can happen in our lives as well: God can speak to our inmost depths. In fact, we should expect to hear his voice in our hearts, the place where God meets us. Jesus said of the Spirit of God, "He lives with you and will be in you" (John 14:17). Indeed, the scriptures speak of the Spirit convicting and instructing our hearts. Paul writes how God's Spirit comforted and encouraged him and even expressed tenderness for Paul in his heart (Philippians 2:1).

This Life Within is our eternal life, which we have already begun to enjoy. John 15 describes it as the quiet yet steady flow of a life-giving sap within a vine. Abiding in Christ, we experience the flow of God's eternal life within us.

Abiding. It's a vintage English word which possesses rich connotations — suggesting being, dwelling, waiting and resting all at the same time.

Listening prayer is abiding prayer: it is having an attitude of attentive listening to God as we live in Christ. There is no real method to it as this comes naturally to us as we come alive to God. Once we were insensitive to God; now, we can hear God more and more as we walk in a just, merciful and humble way before God (Micah 6:8).

But keep in mind that the real goal of listening prayer is not to hear something — it is to be attentive to Someone. We should not be discouraged if we spend time listening to God and "hear nothing." What is important is that our hearts are tuned to God. When God chooses to speak, we will be able to listen.

In listening prayer, many people like to ask God a specific question and then to wait for an answer. The prophet Habakkuk did this in Scripture. He specifically asked God to explain why the Babylonians invaders had come. "Why do you tolerate the treacherous?" he asked God (Habakkuk 1:13). And then he said, "I will look to see what he will say to me" (2:1). After listening to God, he received an answer.

As we watch and wait on God, we may have God speak to us through Scripture, but God might also use our thoughts, conversations and events. Sometimes, God chooses not to reply. But if God does choose to speak to our hearts, we still must test that word. As 1 Thessalonians 5:21 says, "Test everything. Hold on to the good." Spiritual discernment is needed.

Spiritual Discernment

Listening prayer should never be taught apart from spiritual discernment. Many evangelicals in the "listening prayer movement" are enthusiastic about rediscovering this form of prayer, but they do not always teach the place of spiritual discernment. There is a reason why spiritual formation writers from past centuries have warned that private words are the *least* authoritative way of understanding the mind of God. We may hear God speak, but for us to hear God properly, we must know how to practice spiritual discernment.

Spiritual discernment is a process of learning to distinguish between the voices of Satan, the self and the Spirit of God. This requires, above all, humility. It is easy for us to manufacture a "word" about what we think God is saying to us. We need to heed Jeremiah's warning: "Everyone's own word becomes their oracle and so you distort the words of the living God" (Jeremiah 23:36).

Spiritual discernment guards us from foolish delusions. The mission world is full of examples of those who claimed to have direct guidance with disastrous results. This is why Paul warns us to weigh prophecies carefully (1 Corinthians 14:29) and not to be "puffed up with idle notions" (Colossians 2:18). The Desert Fathers were also extremely cautious about mental images and visions. They actively warned novices *not* to pay attention to such images, even if they seemed to be of divine origin, until they learned to be spiritually discerning. Their writings record tragic stories of monks who had fallen into delusions.

Many people who engage in listening prayer practice spiritual discernment by keeping a prayer journal in which they record their holy musings. Over time, as they reflect on what they felt they heard, and as they continue to study Scripture and listen to sound counsel, they begin to discern what is truly from God. We grow in spiritual discernment as we humbly seek the counsel of others in the Body of Christ.

Discernment also requires us to understand the nature of God as taught in the scriptures. God is compassionate and gracious, slow to anger and abounding in love and faithfulness, forgiving yet also exacting (Exodus 34:6-7). God's character is distinctly redemptive (Luke 6:27-36). So, if we hear a "voice" that is cruel, or unnaturally demanding, or which orders us to do something unloving or unwise, we will know immediately that it is not from God and should be rejected. Counterfeit words will also tell us do things that appeal to our pride and our desire for attention, or they will cause us to despair or they will try to damage our witness by making us do foolish things. Any supposed word that strengthens sin in our life is not from God. True words from God always strengthen us in the fruit of the Spirit (Galatians 5:22-23).

Spiritual discernment also requires us to tell the truth. Since Satan is the father of lies, if we harbor deceit, we cannot practice spiritual discernment. Hearing God's Voice means we must live in uttermost truth.

Ignatius is also helpful in warning us about the need to practice discernment during the "afterglow," which is the warm feeling we have after a comforting spiritual experience. He writes that, in this state, "the soul often makes different resolutions and plans which are not the direct result of the action of God." These decisions "have to be very carefully scrutinized before we can give them complete credit and put them into effect."[1]

We need also to remember that sometimes our passivity and timidity makes us unable to discern God's voice. God might be calling us to do something bold and daring but we immediately dismiss it because it seems so difficult. We forget that the greatest mission work happens when God calls us to leave our comfort zones and to launch out in faith.

When we become sensitive to God, we certainly should expect to experience the Life Within. There will be times when the Spirit prompts us, warns us, places burdens on our hearts, or speaks a word to the depths of our souls. This is part of being a godly servant, but we also need to practice spiritual discernment so we can be reasonably certain that when we hear the still, small voice, we will do so in a safe and sure way.

5
Contemplative Prayer

A s our sensitivity to the living God increases, so will our desire
to worship. When we become aware of who God is, what
God is doing and what God means to us, our natural response will
be to offer praise and thanksgiving.

Contemplative prayer is a non-verbal style of praying which
enhances our worship by making us more sensitive to the
movements of God's Spirit within us. When we practice
contemplative prayer, we gaze at God in wonder and our hearts
repose in him. A good example of contemplative prayer is found in
Psalm 27. There, David speaks of gazing on the beauty of the Lord:

> **Psalm 27: 4** *One thing I ask from the LORD, this only do I seek:*
> *that I may dwell in the house of the LORD all the days of my life, to*
> *gaze on the beauty of the LORD and to seek him in his temple.*

Outside, David knows there is trouble. Enemies are waiting to
slit his throat and an army is hunting him down, yet David has
found confidence in God because he has been with God.
Contemplative prayer has the capacity to drain our deepest fears as
it fills our hearts with the vision of God. Psalm 27:5 – "For in the
day of trouble he will keep me safe in his dwelling."

Properly speaking, Christian contemplation is not an activity that
we do in our own effort, but rather it's our heart's inward vision of
God. Contemplation is a form of prayer in which we do not talk to
God so much as we enjoy God for whom he is. Teresa of Avila
described it simply as "nothing else than a close sharing between
friends; it means taking time frequently to be alone with him whom

we know loves us." [1] Others have called it a loving gaze on God, a silent love, or a gaze of faith.

A good way to enter into this form of Christian spirituality is first to remember God in the midst of all we do. Sometimes what separates us from God is not our sins but our distractions from God. In a place with the least interruptions, bring your problems, worries and cares to God and commit them into his hands. Rest yourself in God's love for you. Worship does not begin by ignoring life's concerns; it begins by bringing those concerns to God and resting them in God's love.

Perhaps you might quietly think about a verse or two, or think about the signs of God's love which you experienced that day. Perhaps you might confess to the Lord something that has been troubling you. The goal is to break through the "worry-barrier" and the "busy-ness barrier." This might take just a few minutes, or it could take much, much longer. Once we set aside our distractions, we become more able to focus on God's actions and presence. We are not simply trying to make ourselves calm; we are trying to become more attentive to God.

The next step in contemplative prayer is *meditation*. It is filling our minds with who God is: God's character, words and ways as found in Scripture. We remind ourselves, "God is my heavenly Father who cares for me. He is my Sovereign Lord who is larger than my problems, the Sufferer whose pain redeems this world." We read Scripture to remember what God is like.

With time, our biblical meditation will lead naturally into a contemplative gazing at God in which our efforts begin to be less important and God begins to take more of the initiative in the process. Meditation on Scripture produces contemplation in our souls: the spark creates the holy fire. We have filled our minds with who God is, now we begin dwelling on those thoughts. Contemplation is sitting back and enjoying God's beauty in our hearts. His glory. His splendor. His loving, forgiving nature. His holiness. We just sit there and let the clock tick away. We sit and allow God's Spirit to remind us how Christ died for our sins ... and that God is calling us to a beautiful place ... and how we will live there in God's presence for eternity ... and what is there to fear? What is there to be afraid about, anyways?

We sit there and the words of a hymn might come to mind like:

Amazing grace, how sweet the sound, that saved a wretch like me.... when we've been there ten thousand years, bright shining as the sun, there's no less days to sing God's praise than when we first begun.

As we think about those words and let them sink into our hearts, something happens to us. Fear begins to give way to faith. God's Spirit speaks to our deepest needs.

Those of us who practice contemplative prayer know that they are not there alone, but that God is a part of the process. There's an interaction that goes on as the Spirit of God speaks to our sins, fears, doubts and despairs. The solitude becomes filled with God.

In contemplative prayer, the Spirit might also give us discernment and wisdom. Back in Psalm 27, David prayed, "Teach me your way, O Lord; lead me in a straight path because of my oppressors." One misstep and they were sure to pounce on him. David needed wisdom to know how to escape. He expected help.

In this way, a regular practice of contemplative prayer can greatly aid missionaries, especially during times of crisis or discouragement. In contemplative prayer, the Spirit speaks to our pain and fears and weaknesses and helps us to regain trust in God's sufficiency. Scripture recounts how David once was, "greatly distressed because the men were talking of stoning him ... but David found strength in the LORD his God" (1 Samuel 30:6). When we gaze upon the beauty of the Lord, we find a perfect shelter in the midst of our perfect storms.

Contemplative prayer is usually something that we do alone, but it can also be something that we do together. A group of friends, for instance, may agree to be with God alone in the morning, and then come together to share and pray over lunch. I have experienced such times and have often seen us give each other highly appropriate words of wisdom that seem to come from God as a result of the contemplative hours.   In a similar way, in one particularly low point in my life, when I was preoccupied with worry, a friend sat with me and reminded me who God is. This person read scripture after scripture about God's character and his ways. It was a kind of forced-fed mediation, but it worked and snapped the vicious cycle of worry.

Ignatian Prayer

Ignatius of Loyola is a Catholic spiritual formation writer most known for his work called the *Spiritual Exercises*. His approach to prayer did not originate with him; rather, it reflects the practices of prayer common among Benedictine and Franciscan monks of his time. Many evangelical Christians are beginning to discover these forms of praying. From a Protestant perspective, there is much to interact with and learn from Ignatian prayer, despite any perceived weaknesses.

Ignatius preserved Evagrious' ancient concept of prayer as communing with God in the depths of our hearts. He taught that there can be no real prayer without the grace of God being active at every stage. For this reason, the Ignatian way of prayer first tries to train people to recognize the movements of God's Spirit within them. A great deal of emphasis is placed on the importance of preparing our hearts to pray. Ignatius said that, when we pray, we don't simply start talking to God; rather, we first learn to make our hearts alive and responsive to God. And when we pray, we are to do so with reverence and attentiveness.

Keep in mind, he was serving the medieval Roman Catholic Church in which rote prayers were the norm. In contrast, Ignatius encouraged people to adopt what he calls an "attitude of generosity toward God," in which we just throw ourselves onto God with abandonment and enthusiasm so that we center our affections and attachment on God alone. To pray in the Spirit, we must train our hearts to be attentive to God.

After this preparation, Ignatius then taught people to pray by pondering slowly over themes such as our own sinfulness, or the Ten Commandments, or the Seven Deadly Sins, or the reality of hell. Or, one can take a known prayer such as the Lord's Prayer and think about each word over an extended period of time. We are free to choose our own devotional topics as well.

The goal is inner internalization. Ignatius was trying to break through the rote-filled world of his time to encourage people to develop a warm and personal understanding of the things of God.

One principle he taught seems particularly helpful. As people did their meditative praying, Ignatius advised them to dwell on the things that seemed to speak to them the most. We can hear Ignatius saying, "Do not be in a hurry. One of the main purposes of this kind of praying is to grow more sensitive to the movements of God's Spirit in your hearts. Do so by focusing on those aspects of your meditative praying that seem most meaningful to you."

Another significant thing that Ignatius did was to encourage people to use their imaginations and their senses while praying. For instance, he gave people permission to imagine themselves being in a Bible story and playing a part in it. You are with Jesus in the boat on the Sea of Galilee. A storm arises and threatens the boat. What is it like? Are you afraid of the huge waves? What are you thinking as you try to bail out the water? How does it all speak to you?

Again, his goal was simply to encourage people to develop a tender and warm relationship with Christ. Prayer is a dialogue with God, Ignatius taught. We should then expect God to speak to us in different ways, even by using our imaginations.

Infused Contemplative Prayer

From Evagrious' definition of prayer as "communion of our hearts with God," we have seen that there are as many varieties of prayer as ways we relate to God. We have also seen that there also are non-verbal forms of prayer, and that God sometimes takes the initiative in our prayer relationship with him.

Those who practice contemplative prayer say there are times when God seems to take *almost all* the initiative. Catholic spiritual formation writers call this "infused contemplative prayer." It is not something that we do; it just happens, solely as a gift of grace as we dwell on the beauty of God. It's a non–verbal, loving awareness of God that burns like a holy fire in our hearts and that gradually enters our lives and may even eventually replace discursive prayer. Sometimes, visions or words of knowledge (which Catholic writers call "locutions") accompany it. Thomas Dubay considers infused contemplation as common only among "those who try to live the whole Gospel wholeheartedly and who engage in an earnest prayer life." [2]

Contemplative and Workplace Spiritualities

For centuries, people have felt that contemplation is superior to action. Since at least the time of Eusebius (c. 263 – c. 339), the story of Mary and Martha in Luke 10:38-42 has been interpreted in a way that denigrates workplace spirituality. Mary, who listens quietly to Jesus does the "right thing," while Martha, who works in the kitchen, is seen as being "unspiritual." Eusebius taught that Christ allows us two ways of life: the "perfect life," which is dedicated to contemplation and is available to such spiritual elites as priests and monastics, while the "permitted life" is for the rest of us in the ordinary world. Eusebius believed in a spiritual hierarchy.

In the story of Mary and Martha, however, Jesus does not imply that prayer is superior to work; rather, he is pointing out the needy state of Martha's heart. He does not tell Martha, "Get out of the kitchen!" Rather, he encourages her to focus on God. She had become too obsessed with the meal. Eusebius' interpretation was simply wrong.

In 1520, the Protestant reformer Martin Luther (1483 – 1546) applied the needed corrective. In his *Babylonian Captivity of the Church*, Luther writes: "The works of monks and priests ... do not differ in the least in the sight of God from the works of the country laborer in the field or a woman going about her household tasks." In other words, all work is equal if it is done out of love for God. The person who prays for a living is not superior to the person who works for a living — if both love God. Interestingly, there's a story from the very beginning of the monastic movement that affirms the same thought. St. Antony of Egypt (c. 293-373 AD) was the main initiator of the monastic movement. One day, God revealed to him that there was someone more holy than he. The Spirit of God then led Antony to a woman doing her household chores. As Antony looked at her, it was suddenly revealed to him that she was that holier person.

Eusebius' false dichotomy between prayer and work explains why Protestant missionaries often react negatively to contemplative spirituality. Missionaries are often task-orientated people. We tend to be psychologically wired for action more than contemplation. I have often heard comments such as, "Contemplative praying is impractical. I don't have the time to pray like that."

Actually, contemplative spirituality is more a matter of love than of time. There is something very valuable to it, if we properly understand it. Instead of worrying about the quantity of our prayers, we should focus on the quality of our relationship with God. When we approach our spirituality like this, it affirms our "work in the kitchen" because we know we will also "sit at Jesus' feet" when we need.

Action-orientated leaders need a spirituality that works for them. We find it, not by feeling guilty because we do not pray in a retreat center all day. We find it by keeping our hearts fresh with God. If our work begins to affect our relationship with God, then we know we need to seek personal renewal. But if our hearts are right with God, then our work itself will naturally become a form of prayer. This is what St. Benedict meant when he taught, "To work is to pray." And this, too, is the central idea behind a workplace spirituality.

Today, we have some excellent evangelical authors, such as Richard Foster, who are helping us to learn about contemplative prayer. The classic source which describes the contemplative spirituality of the Desert Fathers and Mothers is called *The Philokalia*, which is well-worth exploring, especially the first volume. St. Teresa of Avila with her book, the *Interior Castle* and St. John of the Cross with his book, *Dark Night of the Soul*, are two other major sources for understanding contemplative prayer. However, if you want something more easily accessible, simply access the Wikipedia article titled "Christian Contemplation."

6

The Providence of God

F or one of its assigned tasks, the Hubble Space Telescope was pointed in the direction of deep space where no stars could be seen. Its powerful lense was focused on a tiny portion of deep space, as wide as a small coin would appear to us from a distance of 20 meters. The lense was then left open for ten whole days — literally staring at nothing — to gather what light it could from distant reaches. After ten days, the exercise revealed over 1500 new galaxies representing billions of stars. Deep space, we learned, is immense.

When some people think of the universe, they conclude, "Matter and energy is all there is, or has been, or ever will be." We call this view, materialism. It says that everything just is, without any absolute beginning or ending or purpose.

Scripture has a different view of reality. It teaches that God not only created the world but continues to be involved in it by preserving it and directing it toward the fulfillment of an ultimate purpose. We call the continued involvement of God in the world, the *providence of God*.

The English word *providence* comes from the Latin *prōvidēre* — from *prō* "beforehand" + *vidēre* "to see." The idea is that God sees in advance and provides what is needed. In Scripture, when God tells Abraham to sacrifice Isaac but then provides a ram for the sacrifice, Abraham recognizes God's providence at work. He calls the place of sacrifice, *Yahweh yireh*, which literally means "the LORD sees" and is usually translated as "the LORD provides."

God sees ahead and provides for us and the entire universe in three major ways:

God Preserves — The world continues to exist solely by God's unceasing involvement. As it says in Revelation 4:11, "For you created all things, and by your will they were created and have their being."

God Enables — God's power makes possible all natural operations and every human choice. Acts 17:28 — "For in him we live and move and have our being."

God Governs — God directs all events toward the fulfillment of his ultimate purpose. "For from him and through him and for him are all things" (Romans 11:36).

All three of these are necessary for there to be a Christian view of reality. If we say, for instance, that God brought the world into existence but no longer cares for it or guides it — that would be Deism, not Christianity. Christian teaching affirms that God is not an absentee parent. We can expect to experience the providential care of our heavenly Father.

Today, it is important to affirm the biblical teaching about providence because secularism deeply affects the thinking of many people. Even for Christian missionaries, a lingering secularism may prevent us from trusting in our heavenly Father as we should.

Three Stories about Providence

Years ago, our family went to the Middle East to serve God. Things often went wrong and there was never enough of the basic supplies. We had to learn not to worry like Americans usually do over such shortages. God had to teach us to trust in his care.

We lived in a quaint little home, but it turned out to be a place of sickness for us. One illness followed unremittingly after another. One day, we almost died all together from carbon monoxide poisoning. That was followed by a procession of viruses, then by giardiasis (a bad intestinal infection). After that, I came down with hepatitis. We were completely worn out by then and did not know what to do. We were supposed to move the next day and I had to buy furniture and load boxes, yet I could not manage to walk up a few stairs.

In our discouragement, we desperately prayed, "God, please help us!" Instantly, I was healed, right then and there. The next day, I literally walked ten miles, bought all the furniture and moved everything. To this day, I know I had hepatitis because my blood still contains the antigens that reacted to it. When I was healed, God spoke these words to my heart: "If your health depends on Me, so does your ministry."

On another occasion, I took a trip on a ship named *Al Tahra*, from the Sinai Peninsula to Aqaba, Jordan. While on the ship, God suddenly spoke to my heart that one day that very ship would sink. So, I prayed for the people who would go through that terrible experience.

The sinking happened about three years later, in 1991. It was one of the worse ferry disasters in Egyptian history. Many people lost their lives, but by God's mercy about 100 came safely to shore. The account of the tragedy, which I kept from a Cairo newspaper dated 18 December 1991, tells of one unusual sign of grace:

Witnesses reported that one survivor was brought to the shore by two Red Sea dolphins, which kept his head above water, warded off sharks and danced with joy on the surface of the sea when he arrived safely on shore.

Having been moved to pray three years earlier, I believe that God was helping people that day.

On another day, I went to the city of Jerusalem to do research as a part of my work. While there, I wanted to visit some friends since it would be the last time I would see them. I was staying overnight in an Arab hotel. In the morning, I asked the owner for directions to my friends' apartment, but his face turned pale when he learned that they were living in a dangerous area. "It's not safe for you to go there on foot," he said. He tried to dissuade me, but then he said, "OK, I'll give you the directions. Here they are ... "

I did not know it, but he purposely gave me the wrong directions, sending me into another part of the city, into a safe area far from my destination. He meant to hopelessly confuse me to keep me safe. Oblivious to his purpose, I followed his incorrect directions perfectly. "Go down this street, then that street, then when you see this building on your right, go up the stairs and you'll find a plaza with some shops. Go into one of the shops and ask for your building."

But God had a different plan. I found that his random directions actually made sense. They actually led me to a plaza, just as I had been told. I walked into one of the shops, miles from my destination, and asked the woman behind the counter about my two friends. She gave me a startled look. "They live right next door to me, but that's miles from here!" She couldn't believe that I had just walked into her store, a complete stranger, and asked where I could find her neighbors.

After she wrote down the address for me, I jumped into a taxi and reached their apartment just a couple of minutes late. Later in the day, when I returned to the Arab hotel and the owner asked me, "Did you find the place?" — he gave me another strange look as I told him, "Your directions were perfect!"

God was teaching me lessons about providence.

Two Ways We Can Live

Jesus teaches us to live our lives with a sense of God's providential care, each and every day. God provides for our existence and our lives more than we realize. He said:

Matthew 6:25-34 Therefore I tell you, do not worry about your life, what you will eat or drink; or about your body, what you will wear. Is not life more than food, and the body more than clothes? Look at the birds of the air; they do not sow or reap or store away in barns, and yet your heavenly Father feeds them. Are you not much more valuable than they? Can any one of you by worrying add a single hour to your life?

And why do you worry about clothes? See how the flowers of the field grow. They do not labor or spin. Yet I tell you that not even Solomon in all his splendor was dressed like one of these. If that is how God clothes the grass of the field, which is here today and tomorrow is thrown into the fire, will he not much more clothe you—you of little faith? So do not worry, saying, 'What shall we eat?' or 'What shall we drink?' or 'What shall we wear?' For the pagans run after all these things, and your heavenly Father knows that you need them. But seek first his kingdom and his righteousness, and all these things will be given to you as well. Therefore do not worry about tomorrow, for tomorrow will worry about itself. Each day has enough trouble of its own.

In these words, Jesus is talking about two ways we can live. *We can live by seeing signs of our heavenly Father's care everywhere.* Our Father watches over his creation. He's nurturing it, providing for it and caring for it. When we view the world like this, it affects how we live. We begin to trust in our heavenly Father. Even when bad things happen, we know God will never forsake us. We may be hard-pressed, but we need not despair. There will always be hope because, Scripture says, "your Father has been pleased to give you the kingdom" (Luke 12:32).

The second way we can live our lives is to choose not to see signs of our heavenly Father anywhere. We look, and all we see is the cold harshness of the world without any hint of a heavenly Father watching over his creation. When we view the world in this way, it also affects how we live. We sense there is no caring presence, no one in heaven to trust and no one to whom we can pour out our hearts in times of need. As a result, we often begin worrying because we're not in God's care. We're all alone.

Stop Worrying!

In Matthew 6, Jesus contrasts these two ways of looking at the world and he tries to jolt us out of the one and into the other. He first tells us plainly, "Do not worry about your life." In the Greek, the verb there is an imperative: "Stop worrying."

Life is filled with lots of little worries every day. If we're supposed to be at work at 8, we can't saunter in at 10 and say, "I don't worry." But Jesus is talking about something different. The Greek word here is *merimnao* — referring to an obsessive worry that eats away at us and makes us forget about the care of our heavenly Father. Jesus orders us to put an end to this kind of worry so that we can live under God's providence. Neurotic worrying does us no good. It just makes us more worried.

Start Seeing!

Not only does Jesus tell us to stop worrying obsessively, he also commands us to start seeing the goodness of God by dwelling intentionally on it. "Consider the birds of the air," Jesus said. "They neither sow nor reap nor store away in barns, and yet your heavenly Father feeds them. Are you not much more valuable than they?" Every day, God showers his goodness on the birds. If they recognize it, why can't we?

One of the main goals of spiritual formation is to help us become more mindful of God's love around us. It is a capital mistake for a missionary to begin focusing on everything that goes wrong, as we so easily can do. Instead, we are to consciously develop the habit of enjoying God's goodness in all events. Perhaps this is why so many of the long-term missionaries I have known have developed a good sense of humor.

It's also important to recognize that our best opportunities to do God's work often come through the setbacks we experience.

I have a friend who went to Bangladesh to plant a church. He succeeded, but it happened through a misfortune. One night, he was mistaken in a dimly-lit village for being a thief and was beaten severely. Only afterwards did the villagers recognize him as the "foreign teacher." My friend could have created enormous trouble for those villagers by bringing the authorities down on them. Instead, when he returned to that village after recovering from his wounds, he forgave them. His act of forgiveness, which the villagers simply could not comprehend, opened their hearts to the Gospel and caused a church to be born.

Meanwhile, another mission worker in the same country suffered another misfortune. In his case, he had his camera stolen. He reacted in a totally different way from my friend. He said, "That's it! I've had enough! I'm leaving this country forever!" And that's what he did.

One person had a misfortune and started a church. The other left the country. And it all depended on their understanding of providence. My friend allowed God to work through his misfortune.

In the long-run, how we respond to evil becomes more important than the evil itself. We can either allow the evil to affect us, or we can set a new course in motion. A perfect example is the story of Joseph in Genesis. He suffered great harm at the hand of his brothers, but this did not worsen him. Joseph did not wallow in self-pity or bitterness or turn judgmental. Instead, he accepted what happened and made the best of the situation. His response allowed God to work providentially through his circumstances for good. When we respond to evil by placing ourselves into God's providential care, God works.

The Prayer of Surrender

In spiritual formation, there is something called the *prayer of surrender*. This is a prayer of trust in the providence of God. When we say a prayer of surrender, we give our lives into God's loving care for situations beyond our control. We express trust in God to work even through the harm. The Coptic Orthodox Church, which I served in Egypt, uses a prayer of surrender in its daily prayer liturgy. The prayer goes:

> *We thank you in any event, for every event and in all events; for you have helped us. … Grant us to pass this holy day and all the days of our life in perfect peace in the fear of your name.*

In the missionary life there are many things beyond our control. Sometimes we find ourselves having to submit to choices that we would not otherwise make. When we willingly trust in God's providence by saying a prayer of surrender, it allows us to experience God in a new way. Even our Lord prayed a Prayer of Surrender on the cross, in hope of the resurrection: "Into your hands I commit my spirit."

The Prayer of Surrender is particularly helpful in the healing of our inner brokenness. When we face difficult circumstances beyond our control, our shadow side makes us react with fear, worry, insecurity and frustration. But when we commit ourselves in trust to God, this vicious cycle is interrupted and breaks and we become more whole inside. Instead of allowing our animal natures to control us, we quietly trust in providence to work. Prayers of surrender are essential in missionary spirituality.

Providence and Evil

For many people, but perhaps not so much for missionaries, suffering is a major reason why they do not believe in God's providential care. "How could a good God allow us to suffer and endure hardship and evil?" Although this has not been a major problem among the missionaries I have known, I will tell one story about suffering and providence.

When I was a chaplain, I supported a man who was dying of cancer. He had a real peace about him so I asked him, "Where did you get this peace from?" He told me that years before his wife was also dying of cancer when an angel suddenly appeared to her at the foot of their bed. He said, "The angel did not say anything but from that moment my wife experienced deep peace. She lived with that peace until she died months later because God gave her hope despite her cancer. And the peace my wife found," said this man, "has lingered on into my life as well."

We do not know why bad things happen, but we know that evil does not disprove providence. Evil happens. Satan attacks. But this does not separate us from God's love. God still works in us and through us despite the evil we endure.

For missionaries, the evil which may try us the most is martyrdom. I have personally known three missionary martyrs. Such deaths should not make us disbelieve in God's love since not a sparrow falls to the ground outside our Father's care (Matthew 10:29). Instead of fearing evil, or worrying about it, or asking why it happens, Jesus calls us to surrender ourselves to providence.

We know that the Christians who were living under the pagan Roman Empire church habitually trained themselves to be prepared for martyrdom. That should be a part of our missionary spirituality as well. We should prepare ourselves to pay the ultimate sacrifice if God so calls us to it. We cannot do the kind of work we do, in the kind of places we do it, without some of us sacrificing our lives.

Micro-faith Christians

So, there are two ways of seeing and living life: under God's providential care, or not. One is the Christian way. The other is the secular way.

We have to ask ourselves, "which way describes me?" If we're honest, we'll probably answer, "I'm somewhere in the middle. I believe in God, yet I often feel anxious."

Yet, when we are like this, Jesus chides us with a choice word. He calls us *mikro-pistoi*. Literally, in the Greek that means *micro-faiths*. It is usually translated, "you who are of little faith" (Matthew 6:30). "You Micro-faiths! Don't you believe?!?" Micro-faith Christians do not trust in God's providential care like Jesus expects them to.

Jesus used that word of poor people living on the edge of survival who might not have sufficient food or clothing for their children. If Jesus commanded people like that to stop worrying obsessively and to stop being *Micro-faiths*, what would he say about us and our worries?

I once knew a missionary who went to the store to buy a can of *crushed* pineapple. But the store carried only *sliced* pineapple. She got really upset. "That stupid store!" she said, "They sell only sliced pineapples, not crushed!" We can get so worked up over such little things. What would Jesus say to us who have so much?

Petition and Intercession

In our relationship with God, Jesus gave us permission to ask about our basic needs from the God of providence when he taught us to pray, "Give us this day our daily bread." Petition is like a child asking a father to provide for something. When we petition God, we are not pleading or manipulating but rather resting in God's will. We know that not all our wants will be met in this decaying world and that our real hope is with God. Living under providence means that we are trusting in the ultimate goodness of God for us. No matter what may happen to us in this world, we know that all will be well in the end.

Similarly, intercession, or praying for the needs of others, is also best done when we hold a firm belief in providence. Modern secularism makes us rely too much on our own strength to do God's work. We forget that God really does chose to work synergistically with us in this world. Looking back on my own years of service, I wish I had done more intercessory praying. Every time I took it seriously, there was more power. In speaking of intercessory prayer, James 5:15 emphasizes, "The prayer of a righteous person is powerful and effective."

God especially wants us to intercede for the salvation of others, so we should allow the Spirit to burden us to pray in this way. I once sat under Dr. Chang Lit-Sen, who had been a leader in China in the early 20th century and then became a Christian seminary professor. One day, he told us in class that he had been burdened for 20 years for his friend, Chang Kuo Tao, to become a Christian. Chang Kuo Tao was one of the original founders of the Communist Party in China but Mao expelled him in a power struggle. I remember the day when Dr. Chang told us, "I visited my friend, Chang Kuo Tao, in Toronto, Canada, and after 20 years of interceding for him, he has now come to faith in Jesus!" That was in 1978, a year before Chang Kuo Tao died. Chang Lit-Sen deeply cared for his old friend, Chang Kuo Tao, and did not cease praying for him to come to Christ. Intercessory prayer works through love.

Teaching Missionary Children about Providence

In the modern era, secularism has weakened our belief in providence. This is true even for missionaries. That is why missionary parents might also want to make sure that they teach their children about God's providence. One way is to present it as a challenge.

I remember telling some teenagers, "You can experience God for yourself. Try it as an experiment. Talk to God in the morning about your day. Tell him whatever worries you. Ask him to give you help and wisdom for all the important things you will be facing that day. Whatever it is, talk to God, surrender your day into God's hands and then at the end of the day think back and see how God helped you." I was simply teaching them about petition with an emphasis on God's providence.

In the group, only one young woman accepted my challenge. The next week, she came back with a big smile on her face and said, "It actually works! I experienced God helping me all day long! I couldn't believe it." A few years later I met her one day after she went off to university. The first thing she told me was, "I'm still doing what you taught me and it's totally changed my life. I'm continuing to experience God every day."

Missionary parents usually have a deep personal relationship with God, which is one reason why they became missionaries in the first place, but their children do not necessarily have the same experience. The faith of the children of earnest Christians begins as a hand-me-down faith that may be less personal. Children are brought to church and taught the faith of their parents, but this can lead to a legalistic perspective of God, filled with obligations and lacking in love and joy. Even when we teach our children to call God, "Father," they may not know what that means. Yet, when we encourage our children to experience the God of providence, it helps them to develop a personal faith in God.

This is one reason, when I teach about providence to missionaries, I ask them to share their own stories and to continue to do so in their future conversations. Our children need to hear our stories about God's providential care.

7

Spiritual Disciplines

S piritual formation is based on the idea of discipline. We are not just believers, we are disciples — *disciplined believers* — who live under the discipline of Christ. We are to incorporate into our lives spiritual disciplines that will challenge us, prod us, remind us and enable us to grow spiritually.

What is a Spiritual Discipline?

A spiritual discipline is any activity through which God works to strengthen our spiritual lives. Just as the discipline of practicing keyboard scales improves our skill at playing the piano, so spiritual disciplines — such as worship and Bible reading — help us to grow spiritually. Paul reminds us to be spiritually disciplined when he says in 1 Timothy 4:7, "Train yourself to be godly."

There is a difference between *training* and *trying*. We can try to play the piano by pecking at a song, but then we realize it is harder than we thought so we give up. When we train ourselves to play the piano, however, we are more serious. We enter a program of instruction and follow the steps needed until we learn to play properly.

Likewise, to succeed at dieting, we need a program that trains us. We can try a crash diet but it inevitably fails — leading to guilt and frustration. One reason why twelve-step programs are successful is because they follow a training approach to transformation. Good models of spiritual formation also follow a training approach.

Christ's Call to Discipleship

The fullest form of Jesus' call to discipleship is found in Matthew 11:28-30:

> *Come to me, all you who are weary and burdened, and I will give you rest. Take my yoke upon you and learn from me, for I am gentle and humble in heart, and you will find rest for your souls. For my yoke is easy and my burden is light.*

In his invitation, Christ differentiates his discipleship from that of the Pharisees. They tried to keep themselves separate from sin by following strict rules. In contrast, Christ calls us to take his training yoke upon us and learn from him through a gradual training program of transformation.

In the training program which one man gave to his young horses, at first he gently cared for them by brushing them, talking softly to them and giving them treats to eat. Then he gradually started leading them around. Only after he gained their trust and affection did he try to ride them. Increasingly, they learned to love their new life since he matched his training to their abilities and instincts.

In a similar way, Christ trains us under his easy yoke. He invites us to work alongside him to learn from him. It's a partnership in which he does most of the hard work. We feel his energy moving within us and motivating us, even as we serve him. He gives us tasks that match our abilities yet which also challenge us. In Christian discipleship, grace aids effort. It's a training in which we are gradually transformed inside as we make lifestyle decisions, establish goals and learn to serve and even to suffer for Christ.

We have a constant tendency to make our yokes heavier than they are meant to be, just like the Pharisees did. When we first became Christ's disciples, he installed discipleship software into our hearts that ran just fine — Jesus 1.0. Then we installed new software which promised so much — Pharisee 2.0! When we did so, however, something happened and our discipleship began running much more slowly, as if it was under a burden.

Christ is always the Discipler. His yoke is always custom-fitted to us. When we wear someone else's yoke, it will always chafe. Only Christ's yoke works perfectly in our lives. That's why discipleship can never be reduced to following a set of rules or "doing the disciplines." When spiritual disciplines exist in and of themselves, they turn into burdensome laws. Wise spiritual coaches recognize this.

To help in the custom-fitting of Christ's yoke, some evangelical missionaries are now using spiritual directors to help them. In this context, the word *director* means "a guide" since it descends from the old Latin word *dērigere*, to guide. An experienced spiritual director does not impose his or her own ideas about discipleship on another person. Rather, they listen with individuals to try to discern what Christ is saying. As a spiritual director listens with an individual, both are looking to Christ to reveal what might be the best next step to take for the individual's discipleship.

Spiritual directors are aware that our personalities certainly play a role in the custom-fitting. For instance, they know that people with a rich imagination may benefit from visualizing themselves within a biblical story as they read it. Analytical thinkers, on the other hand, will prefer to study the Bible systematically. Extroverts like to pray aloud in groups while introverts like quiet times of private reflection. A wise spiritual director will help each individual to find the spiritual disciplines which best fit their needs, personality and season of life.

Personality tests, such as the Myers-Briggs Type Indicator ® (MBTI ®), help a great deal. Some spiritual formation writers have applied the results of MBTI testing to spirituality, suggesting which spiritual disciplines best fit each type of personality.[1] Awareness of MBTI thinking helps us to avoid basic mistakes in spiritual direction work, such as forcing extroverted mission leaders to adopt spiritual disciplines best suited for introverts.

Spiritual Disciplines as Means of Grace

In Protestant thinking, spiritual disciplines are considered to be *means of grace*. That is, God works through them to strengthen our spiritual lives.

Generally speaking, there are three major means of grace: the Word, the Sacraments and Prayer. These are the "Basic Three." They are known as the *normal means of grace* since they are the normal way by which we grow spiritually.

In addition, Christians through the centuries have also recognized *specialized means of grace*. Generally speaking, these are all the other spiritual disciplines.

For instance, John Wesley, the founder of Methodism, mentioned among the "means of grace" both normal and specialized disciplines:

(1) *Works of Piety*: such as prayer, fasting, Scripture, Holy Communion and Baptism, and

(2) *Works of Mercy*: such as visiting the sick, aiding the needy and working for justice.

In the late 20th century, Richard J. Foster introduced many evangelicals to such spiritual disciplines as fasting, meditation, study, solitude, submission, confession and celebration. Since then, others have complied extensive lists of specialized spiritual disciplines including: simplicity, silence, going on retreats, secrecy, chastity, mentoring, serving, self-examination, hospitality, journaling, scripture memorization, Sabbath-keeping and creation care — to mention just a few.

God can work through these specialized means of grace to strengthen our spiritual lives, but they should never overshadow the "Basic Three" — the Word, the Sacraments and Prayer. While exploring and enjoying the specialized means of grace, we should remember that they are tools for our spiritual edification. Christ our Discipler may call us to use some of them, but he may also call us to use other spiritual disciplines over time.

Bible Reading as a Spiritual Discipline

The main spiritual discipline in the Protestant tradition has always been the reading of Scripture. I once conducted a survey of several hundred people in which I asked two questions: (1) "How much do you read the Bible?" and (2) "How close do you feel toward God?" The relationship in my simple survey proved to be linear: any increase in Bible reading was directly associated with a closer feeling to God.

As missionaries, we tend to know our Bibles, but how can we best enhance our spiritual discipline of Bible reading to promote our own spiritual formation?

We first need to know what the Bible is. Many of us follow a verse-by-verse approach to the Bible. We are familiar with individual verses and stories but we tend to lack a systematic understanding of how the whole fits together.

At its simplest, *the Bible is the story of the self-revelation of God through a chosen people.* God chose a people — Abraham and his descendants — to reveal himself to the world through them.

There are six major chapters in this Story of God's self-revelation to the world: [2]

CREATION: The Lord God created the world and established his reign in it, but humanity rejected its knowledge of God.

ABRAHAM: God made a covenant with Abraham and his descendants to reveal himself again to the world through them.

EXODUS: The descendants of Abraham became the people of Israel. God redeemed Israel from bondage under Pharaoh and reaffirmed his covenant with them as his chosen people.

NATIONHOOD: Israel became a nation under God's reign, but it failed to live for God or tell others what they learned about God as they should have.

EXILE: God sent his rebellious people into exile. The prophets predicted that a remnant would be restored under a righteous servant king who would bring in the true reign of God.

THE COMING OF THE KING: The promised reign finally occurs in Jesus, the Messiah, who announced at the beginning of his ministry, "The kingdom of God is at hand" (Mark 1:15). In Jesus, the self-revelation of God to the world is complete. The Incarnation is the central interpretive principle of the Bible since it fulfills the Story of God.

Once we know what the Bible is, and the framework by which it develops, we are able to understand the context of all the details, characters and subplots of Scripture. Instead of reading passages in isolation, we can begin seeing how each passage reinforces a whole picture. We then are able to profit from the two approaches for reading the Bible: reading for information and reading for transformation.

Reading for Information

When we read the Bible for information, we are trying to understand the original background and meaning of each passage. We use the findings of archaeology, linguistics, sociology, cultural anthropology, literary genres and history to try to reconstruct what a text would have meant to its author and first readers. Although we can never completely succeed at this reconstruction, we can often do so to a reasonable degree.

This approach to reading the Bible also has been called the *historical and grammatical approach*, and the *literal reading* of the Bible. We now have some excellent resources that help us to read the Bible in this way, such as handbooks, readers' commentaries and study

Bibles filled with notes, introductions and paragraph titles. These aids make reading far more informative, productive and enjoyable.

The inductive Bible study method is also based on the literal reading of the Bible. It begins by asking basic observation questions of a text such as: "Who is speaking?" "What is happening?" "When did it happen and where?" This is then followed by interpretive questions like: "Why did it happen and how?" The final step probes the implications for our lives.

When we read the Bible for information, we are trying to understand the context. This protects us from *isogesis* —which is reading our own interpretations into a verse. By reading the Bible in community with the world of scholarship, we safeguard ourselves from this. However, the danger is that our Bible reading will turn into a dry exercise which has no effect on the heart. In the worse cases, we will analyze a text thoroughly but never allow it to speak to us.

Reading for Transformation

Bible information alone will not change our hearts. We also need to read the Bible for transformation. When we do this, we purposefully try to listen to God in our hearts as we read. Since the Bible is the inspired story of the self-revelation of God through a chosen people, we ask God to speak through the text and apply the words to our lives as disciples. We pray for the Spirit of God to illumine the texts to us as we read.

This approach has also been called the *spiritual reading* of the Bible, as compared to a *literal reading*. Today, evangelicals simply call it reading the Bible devotionally.

The evangelical habit of reading the Bible devotionally has ancient roots in a tradition of the Church known as *lectio divina* (LEX-i-oh di-VEE-nuh). The Cathusian writer, Guigo II, who died around 1188, developed lectio divina from much earlier precedents.

In lectio divina, we read a section of Scripture slowly and prayerfully, with special attention paid to the words that appear to speak directly to our discipleship. We then pray about the spiritual truth that has been spoken to us and think about it. Here is a brief outline of lectio divina as it is commonly presented:

LECTIO DIVINA
Reading
Read a passage slowly.

Biblical Meditation
Mull over what seems meaningful.

Prayer
Pray about what you are meditating on.

Contemplation
Abide with what speaks to your heart.

As part of the lectio divina exercise, Guigo also encouraged meditation on the imagery of a text, not just its meaning. Later medieval writers such as Ignatius of Loyola developed Guigo's thinking into sensory exercises in which the participant tries to imagine the original *emotional* setting by picturing themselves within the stories. Some evangelicals are now exploring these sensory exercises in their own devotional reading of the Bible.

Guigo describes the inter-relationship between the four elements of lectio divina (reading, meditation, prayer and contemplation) in this way:

Reading without meditation is barren.

Meditation without reading tends to produce error.

Prayer without meditation is tepid.

Meditation without prayer is unfruitful.

Prayer with devotion produces contemplation.

We might say that he encouraged readers to allow a text to affect their will and their emotions, not just their minds.

The weakness of reading the Bible for transformation is that we can forget the original context, thereby encouraging fanciful interpretations. When evangelicals teach lectio divina, we need to remember this shortfall.

These two styles of reading the Bible are meant to be complementary. Studying the background of the Bible enhances our devotional reading by preserving us from fanciful interpretations, while our devotional reading encourages us to hear God speaking to our hearts from the texts. Together, both help the spiritual discipline of reading the Bible to be a fruitful exercise.

A Life Review Retreat

J ohn Calvin (1509-1564) wrote: "Without knowledge of self, there is no knowledge of God. ... Without knowledge of God, there is no knowledge of self."[1] This basic principle of spiritual formation is called *double knowledge*: our knowledge of God and our knowledge of self are inter-related. As God meets us in the depths of our hearts, we learn the truth about ourselves so that God can gradually change us.

This is why periodic retreats are especially helpful for our spiritual formation. As we seek God in a reflective way, we learn things about ourselves that otherwise might remain hidden.

In preparing this book, I worked with a team that taught spiritual formation to missionaries. Whenever we led a seminar, we always included a "life review retreat" that proved to be very popular. It is an inductive approach in which we ask the Holy Spirit to speak to us through a brainstorming process.[2] Here is how it works:

1. Prayer

Begin, of course, with prayer. Ask God's Spirit to reveal things to you, to guide and to be with you as you do your life review. Enjoy the time with God!

2. "Brainstorm Your Life" (*about 45 minutes*)

What are the significant people, events and circumstances that happened in your life? Write down each memory as it comes to mind, when it comes to mind, on separate pieces of sticky note paper and stick them on a large piece of poster paper. Place the older memories toward one side and the newer memories on the other. I suggest that you use the same color of sticky note paper for this.

3. "Brainstorm" Your Walk with God (*about 30 minutes*)

Following the same pattern as above, brainstorm your relationship with God. Jot down significant events, such as when you felt especially close to God or when you felt there was a crisis in your relationship with God. Freely write down whatever comes to mind on sticky notes. You may wish to use sticky notes having a different color for this than before.

4. Summarize Your Life (*15-30 minutes*)

Reviewing all your notes, group them into different periods of your life, then try to give a descriptive title to each period. For instance, you might call your younger years, "My time growing up in Ghana." You might even try giving a title to the story of your whole life.

5. Reflect (*about 30-45 minutes*)

Using the following questions, as well as your own, reflect on your life. Write down the thoughts that come to mind:

What has brought me closer to God?

What has led me farther from God?

Who has been spiritually significant to me?

What have I done that has been spiritually significant?

What has been painful, but necessary?

Where am I in my relationship with God right now?

What do I want my relationship with God to become?

6. Share *(15-30 minutes)*

Share what you have been learning about yourself with another person. (It is best to undertake this life-review retreat as part of a group.)

7. Understand

Understand that a life-review like this is just a snap-shot of your life, not a comprehensive analysis. Your reflection can be influenced by recent events and pressing issues in your life today. If you were to do another review in the same way at a later time, different insights would emerge. As we engage in spiritual reflection over time, we begin to see a clearer picture of how God has been working in our lives and what God may be calling us to do in the future.

Spiritual Warfare

A s missionaries, we know that spiritual warfare exists but we might not take it as seriously as we should. After all, the enemy is largely unseen so it is easy to dismiss the demonic. Yet, we've also had our experiences.

Once, when I was a pastor, I labored for six years to renew a spiritually dying church. Early on, I asked for the advice of an older pastor whose church had a remarkable awakening. I asked him naïvely, "How did you do it? What's your method?"

He told me of no method. Instead, he forced me to see the unseen. In a calm voice he told a stark story to change my worldview. He mentioned how twice, at critical turns in his church's renewal, a demon appeared to him. It glared at him with seething hatred. He prayed and recited the Apostles' Creed until that evil presence vanished.

"Don't be deceived. The powers of darkness are real," he warned me. "This work is spiritual. Don't get caught by all the petty squabbles in a church. Pray and fast. Focus on teaching the Word. It's Jesus that brings the renewal."

I am thinking about our mission work in the light of his words. How divided we can be! How discouraged we can feel! We now have computers, but do we rely on the power of the Spirit?

A long time ago, in a different mission situation, the power of the Spirit was all that Christians had. The Roman Empire was strong and paganism still rampant. So what did the Christians of that time do? Holy men and women trod into the desert to wage war against the unseen powers. These first Egyptian desert monastics worked out the Church's first systemic thinking about spiritual warfare. In this chapter we will explore their original thoughts in the hope that we might gain insight for today.

The Egyptian Desert

The silence lies heavy in the desert of Egypt . . . so heavy, with no modern mechanical interruptions, nor natural motion of trees, not even the whisper of a breath of wind, that it just develops its own presence. In the desert, the silence is engulfing, so thick that talking seems like an act of violence, like shattering a piece of glass. Being alone in the desert, the loudest sound is the beating of the heart and the Brownian motion of molecules on your eardrum. In this setting, the Desert Fathers and Mothers went to hear the voice of God.

They did so as their world was changing. Pagan Rome was crumbling to the touch of Christianity, but the new faith was also losing its virulence. As conversions to Christ became *avant garde*, the church became increasingly shallow. This caused men and women who hungered for God to drift into the desert, where they could be deep people on their own terms.

The Desert Fathers and Mothers became the spiritual leaders of their time. They remembered Jesus' words, "You are the salt of the earth," and became living reminders of what true salt was supposed to taste like in a world gone insipid. They also left behind for us specific instructions on how to produce Holy Salt for ourselves — instructions on spiritual formation that they summed up in the single Greek word, *theosis*.

What is theosis? It is becoming holy by having a Holy Christ develop within us. Athanasius (293-373 AD) described it using the catchy phrase, "God became man in order that man might become God." He is not saying that we can become divine, only that Christ can form within us. It is participating "in the divine nature" to "escape the corruption in the world" as 1 Peter 1:3-4 phrases it.

The desert monks used the process of theosis to produce Holy Salt within their souls. They fasted. They prayed. Some lived deep in the desert, completely alone. They reflected extensively about their struggle with sin and eventually they formed a theory about spiritual warfare. They thought of it as God's grace forming within us and vanquishing our prevailing sins, one by one, and so giving us authority over Satan.

Evagrious Ponticus (345-399 AD), interviewed these monks who did the original research on the prevailing sins common to humanity. St. John Cassian then took the information and published it throughout the western Roman Empire. Eventually, Cassian's formulation became known to us as the Seven Deadly Sins: pride, gluttony, lust, envy, anger, greed and sloth.

The Desert Fathers and Mothers regarded these prevailing sins as *passions*. Today, we think of a passion as an ardent emotion, but the ancient Greek world considered a passion to be an impulse that controls us, making us passive and helpless to resist its will. In this way, the English words 'passion' and 'passive,' which both come from the Greek word *pathos*, are conceptually linked. The monks taught that when we yield to these passions, we become enslaved to the demonic by gratifying "the cravings of our sinful nature and following its desires and thoughts" (Ephesians 2:1-3). Theosis, then, is a process by which God gradually drives out these prevailing sins through the formation of Christ within us. As God enables us to become free from our besetting sins, we are able to gain authority over Satan. It is in this way that the desert monastics considered spiritual warfare to be intimately tied into a person's spiritual growth.

Walking the Ancient Path

So, how do we walk this ancient path of *theosis* today? First, we must recognize that the Desert Fathers and Mothers were tough desert fighters who were waging a fierce spiritual war. Walking the ancient path with them is to journey into a spiritual battle. They tell us that the very first step is to make a deep and continuing repentance so that we turn from all known sins in our lives. We talked about this already in chapter three.

After this initial repentance, our task is to keep watch — spiritually alert — against temptation. The desert fathers and mothers understood temptation to be a demonic provocation meant to deceive and entrap us by weakening our love for God. They developed a detailed understanding of how these provocations arise. [1] The more we assent to a provocation in our hearts, they taught, the more we become deceived by sin and enslaved by our passions. Yet, if we resist the provocation by the grace of God, we gain discernment and become spiritually stronger.

Their teaching is important for missionaries who live in today's sexualized world. Jesus warns us to keep a careful watch over what is happening in our hearts (Matthew 5:27-30), yet deep psychological needs can compound with our sexual temptations until we feel powerless to change. We may feel too ashamed to talk about our temptations with anyone, but that is what we need to do the most. Member Care personnel who are sensitive to spiritual things and who are trained in the psychological sciences can help us regain our walk with God. Although the Desert Fathers did not have psychologists with them, they were some of the earliest investigators into the workings of the human psyche. They would have welcomed the role of psychology in the battle against Satan.

The Desert Fathers regarded everything that separates us from God to be a demonic temptation which we must reject decisively. As we repent, we renew our love for God and become inflamed with a holy zeal — which is a fire within our hearts that motivates us to work for the purposes of God. To aid this process, the Desert monastics valued spiritual words of wisdom which they received from the Bible and from spiritual guides.

The monastics also used asceticism to help them fight against temptation. The word "asceticism" comes from the Greek word *askesis,* which has to do with athletic exercising. The monks thought of Christian asceticism as being spiritual exercises which strengthen the soul.

Many of us are not very familiar with asceticism. It is a form of prayer in which we invite God to work his grace in our hearts as we express our dependency on God by making ourselves weak in some way. Asceticism usually involves such disciplines as fasting and keeping vigil but it can also include such things as not seeking fame or power. Christian asceticism arose in imitation of Christ, who used the ascetic practice of fasting to battle against temptation and Satan in the desert (Matthew 4:1-11).

The goal of asceticism is always to develop a life of prayer. The goal is not to denigrate the body, as many commonly misunderstand. Since God declared the material world to be good in creation, the body is not in itself evil. Ascetic spiritual disciplines are simply a means to help us grow closer to God. As the Apostle Paul said, "When I am weak, then I am strong" (2 Corinthians 12:10, cf. 1 Cor 9:24-27). By losing strength, the intent is to grow more dependent on God's grace and to increase the presence of Christ within the believer.

The monks noticed that as they grew in the grace of God, their inner passions became stilled and a deep quietness and peace began to permeate their lives.

This is a late stage in the process of theosis, when we become more free from our reigning passions and achieve a state of dispassion — not in the sense that we become disinterested in life, but that we become liberated from the power of our demonic passions and our souls become fully able to love God. The Greek Orthodox Church named this inner stillness: *hesychia*. It's a form of prayer in which we live in communion with God, free from life's idolatries while listening to and communing with God.

It is when we are in this state of deep trust and inner quiet that we are most able to hear the Voice of God and to distinguish it from the voice of self and the voice of Satan. We gain the gift of discernment.

The process of theosis sounds simple, yet the monks considered the journey difficult because sin deceives us so easily. Theosis develops discernment within us, yet it also requires discernment to begin the journey. Since no one possesses spiritual wisdom in the beginning of their journey, the monks required novices to have a spiritual father or mother as their guide — someone who knew the path and the human soul. This is why Anthony the Great (251-356 AD), the founder of Christian monasticism, felt discernment to be the chief virtue, because it makes all the other virtues possible. [2]

This is but a brief, cursory summary of the teaching of the ancient monastics on spiritual growth and spiritual warfare.

Other Emphases

When we turn to the rest of the New Testament, we find two other important emphases.

First, Scripture clearly demonstrates that Christ has decisively defeated the powers of Satan through his atoning death on the cross (Hebrews 2:14-15). Spiritual warfare is not just what we do, but what Christ has already done.

Secondly, Paul's describes spiritual warfare as an activity of the whole church, not just of individuals. This is seen clearly in his image of the Christian soldier, which is meant to apply to the whole church and not just to individuals (Ephesians 6:10-18). Christ's people are meant to work together to defeat the powers of darkness in the world by promoting truth and righteousness (6:14), evangelizing the world (6:15), exercising faith (6:16), resting under God's protection as his children (6:17), studying the Word (6:17) and praying (6:18). These are some of the normal ways by which the Christian Church wages its spiritual warfare.

Besides what we find in the Desert Fathers and in the New Testament, some of the best thinking in recent times about spiritual warfare has come out of the Lausanne movement with their 2000 Nairobi consultation, *Deliver Us from Evil*. Search under "Nairobi 2000 Lausanne." Their material is valuable for mission work.

In an age of technique and technology, we must never forget that the struggle against the spiritual powers of darkness is real. Let us not be satisfied with a superficial spirituality but let us instead deepen our dependency on God and avoid any tendency to secularize our service. For those of us who have families on the field, especially understand that the children of Christian workers are not immune from demonic attack. On the contrary, Satan seems to make a special effort to undermine the tender faith of our children. Pray for your children every day as well as for your work.

Part Two: Community

Community and Spiritual Formation

H oward Hendricks, who taught as an American seminary professor for over fifty years, once reported:

I've never forgotten the time my wife, Jeanne, and I were invited to Thanksgiving dinner with a group of third-year seminary students. Every Thanksgiving seven couples would get together, and they would have a blast! One year they invited Jeanne and me to be their guests. We had a time like I do not think I have ever had in fifty-six years as a seminary professor.

We ate together, we played games, we laughed, we cried, we prayed together, and finally we left to go home. The moment I got into the car I leaned over and announced, 'Sweetheart, if every student training for vocational Christian service were involved in a small group like that, we would reduce the attrition rate to zero.'

From what I understand, that special group continues to meet together as a team on an annual basis. They pray together, they study and think together, they evaluate and hold each other accountable. ... They certainly sealed in my mind the notion that experiencing authentic community is essential for ministry preparation.

In contrast, Hendricks then goes on to describe a study he once undertook of men who had left the ministry for moral lapses. In every interview he conducted, not a single man thought this would ever happen to him. Hendricks then asked each one, 'Tell me about your accountability group.' In reply, not a single man except for one said he had ever participated in such a group. [1]

Being in community is absolutely vital for our spiritual health. It's strange, then, that the emphasis even in so many discipleship and spiritual formation books is on the individual's own spiritual growth. In contrast, the New Testament teaches that spiritual growth primarily happens in community:

> *Ephesians 4:15-16*   *Rather, speaking the truth in love, we are to grow up in every way into him who is the head, into Christ, from whom the whole body, joined and held together by every joint with which it is equipped, when each part is working properly, makes the body grow so that it builds itself up in love.*

Increasingly, in the modern world, we think of ourselves as being *persons* instead of a *people*. Once, as a people, we lived closely together, did things together, and helped one another to survive. Now, we're busy. Our families are smaller. And we spend years working on our personal goals, like obtaining degrees. We have become individuals who have forgotten how to think and act as a people. So, when we hear the "one another" verses of the Bible — like "love one another" and "carry each other's burdens" — they do not speak to us as they once did. And when we hear the pronoun *you* in Paul's letters, we naturally think it refers to the single individual and not to the whole community as Paul intended.

Our breakdown in community affects our spirituality as missionaries. Some of us feel intensely lonely. When we do have mandated meetings, such as monthly team meetings, the fellowship may seem superficial. So often, we never discuss the deeper issues and we never seek healing in our relationships. We privately carry our burdens and feel too busy to carry the burdens of others. Individualism hinders our spiritual formation.

Working against this trend toward individualism is the communal nature of God. The Triune God lives in community: Father, Son and Holy Spirit. This is not just a theological phrase but a description of a vital dynamic. God models for us what it means to live in community, and upon this we can build a healthy spirituality.

Christian Community Begins with God

We say that "God is love" (1 John 4:16). By this we understand that the universe is not coldly materialistic by nature, nor is it ruled by a self-centered autocrat. Love and relationship lie at the very heart of everything. Community exists in the very being of God. Within God there is a constant expression of love, involving relatedness and genuineness, knowing and being known. God is not the Great Alone One. God is a Community of Love.

The New Testament describes this Community of Love as the Father, Son and Holy Spirit. (Matthew 28:19, John 14:26, 2 Corinthians 13:14, Titus 3:4-6 and 1 John 4:13-15). By the fourth century AD, the Church formally defined this relatedness as a tri-unity, or Trinity. Gregory of Nazianzus went a bit further and artistically described God as a Holy Dance. The word he used is *perichorēsis*, from the Greek words for "dance" and "around." More specifically, the perichorēsis of the Trinity is the interweaving and interpenetration of the members of the Trinity. They are One, yet they also indwell each other in complete mutual submission and love. Their Dance is endless and harmonious, united yet distinct — each member of the Trinity serving and honoring the other. Perichorēsis is intimacy. It is fellowship. It is community. "The Father is in me, and I in the Father," Jesus said (John 10:38b).

The communal nature of God becomes the basis for Christian community. The Father, Son and Holy Spirit all honor each other and promote each other's significance. They have perfect trust, submission and mutuality toward one another. Their perfect love is characterized by availability, self-giving and constant interaction. In their Dance, they never step on each other's toes! Likewise, when we come to know God, we instinctively begin to want to reproduce the Holy Dance amongst ourselves. In the body of Christ, we practice humility and agape love. We rejoice and mourn together. We devote ourselves to one another and we honor one another above ourselves. We serve each other and bear one another's burdens, becoming one body.

As we grow spiritually, the perichorēsis of the Trinity also begins to penetrate into our lives as well. Scripture describes us as being "in Christ." It also says that both the Holy Spirit and God the Father are "living" within us (Romans 8:9-16, 1 John 4:15). The Eastern Church calls this presence of God within us, *divinization*, meaning that we are participating in God's communal life.

Our personal experience of this communal life with God is meant to directly influence how we treat each other in the body of Christ. That is why Paul wrote:

> **Philippians 2:1-2** *Therefore if you have any encouragement from being united with Christ, if any comfort from his love, if any common sharing in the Spirit, if any tenderness and compassion, then make my joy complete by being like-minded, having the same love, being one in spirit and of one mind.*

Our Experience of the Father

God the Father loves the world he created. He providentially provides for the world and is leading and guiding it toward an ultimate destiny. He gives us grace to believe and forgives our sins. The Father is the source of everything and for him we are meant to live. The primary way we experience God the Father is through his love for us. "The Spirit himself testifies with our spirit that we are God's children" (Romans 8:16).

When we personally realize that we are loved by God our Father, it speaks to the deepest needs in our lives and begins to replace our insecurities and our excessive desires for money, power and fame. It also changes our motives and values. As God's love does all of these things within us, it heals our hearts and our relationships.

One study done at Rush University Medical Center in Chicago demonstrates the power of the love of God. The study found that patients who strongly knew that God loved them were 75 percent more likely to get better with medical treatment for clinical depression. Researcher Patricia Murphy said this was "tied specifically to the belief that a Supreme Being cared."[2] This is why we have a daily devotional time: to nurture ourselves in the love of God.

Our Experience of the Son

Christ is God Incarnate. Through him, we come to know what God is like. By his death, our sins are atoned and we find peace with God. Jesus is our high priest who continues to intercede for us in prayer. He heals us, redeems us and fulfills us by giving us life abundant. Christ is our brother and our champion. The primary way we experience God the Son is through his grace for us.

When we know that we have been forgiven because Jesus died on the Cross for us, it turns us into people of grace. Just as we have received grace, we want to give grace to others. This imparts a redemptive quality to our relationships.

Redemption is an important cultural implication of Christianity. Because Christ shed his blood for us, we know that human life is valuable. Ultimately, this simple fact prompts us to treat people with respect and dignity.

Many organizations have a *utilitarian* view of people — they use people and then discard them when they no longer fulfill the purposes of the organization. But when we experience the grace of Jesus, it changes our attitude toward people from *utilitarian* to *redemptive*. Instead of asking, "How can I use people for my purposes?" we begin thinking, "How can I develop people as we work together?" Or, "How can I be a blessing to people in the body of Christ who may be very different from me?" Living in God's grace, we learn to offer grace to others.

Our Experience of the Holy Spirit

The Holy Spirit is the Counselor, who lives inside the believer to convict, convert and consecrate us until we are wholly God's. The Spirit strengthens, encourages, empowers and enlivens us. Without the Spirit, we're like sailing ships that lack wind or households without electricity. The Spirit of God also prods, pulls and guides us toward the destiny which God has prepared for us in Christ. The primary way we experience God the Holy Spirit is through the help the Spirit gives us to live for God.

Our experience of the Spirit affects our communal life with other believers in two major ways.

First, the Spirit gives us spiritual gifts so that we may strengthen each other in the body of Christ (Romans 12:3-8, 1 Corinthians 12-13, Ephesians 4:7-16). The Greek word for these gifts of grace is *charismata* — it is God's power working through us to help someone else. We are meant to experience God through each other in the body of Christ, and not just privately.

So, if you had the charismata of encouragement, you would feel drawn to talk to people who are discouraged and overwhelmed. As you interacted with them, they would sense your care for them and they would feel their burdens lifting and joy returning. They might even smile again because of your visit. It is God working through you — using your spiritual gift to help another person. That's one reason Christians need to be in a fellowship together, so that we can give and receive the charismata among each other.

Secondly, our experience of the Spirit also teaches us how to care for others in the body of Christ. The Spirit grieves within us when we are hateful toward others. The Spirit rejoices within us when we are patient, caring and encouraging. In imitation of the Spirit, we become more willing to empower others toward their fulfillment.

Unfortunately, the western Christian understanding of the Holy Spirit has been affected by the *filioque* controversy. This is the somewhat baffling matter in which the Church of Rome added a phrase to the Nicene Creed which says the Spirit proceeds from the Father *and the Son* (*filioque* in Latin). Rome acted on its own when it added the filioque clause, which was a major reason behind the Great Schism of 1054 AD, splitting Christianity into eastern and western churches.

Most missionaries would regard all of this as irrelevant nonsense. Actually, it is very relevant to our spiritual lives.

In effect, the filioque addition demotes the Holy Spirit into being the junior partner of the Holy Trinity. By saying that the Spirit comes from both the Father and the Son, it disturbs the balance within the Holy Dance. In truth, the Father, Son and Spirit are all equal, and each possesses unique traits, but two cannot possess a unique trait at the expense of the third without destroying the balance.

The effect was to weaken the role of the Spirit in western Christianity and so to affect its spirituality. Orthodox scholars argue that this is why so much of Catholic theology is based on philosophy rather than on *theoria*, which is spiritual illumination. In the same way, rationalism has come to replace spiritual illumination within many parts of Protestant Christianity. Within western Christianity, the Spirit is also often described as the love of the Father and the Son for the world — thereby reducing the Spirit to being just a virtue. And it is a historical fact that much of western Protestantism has just simply ignored the Spirit's role for centuries, causing Pentecostalism to arise to try to correct the imbalance.

The filioque controversy teaches us that our understanding of the Trinity directly affects our spirituality. We are meant to experience the Holy Trinity in perfect balance: Father, Son and Spirit. All three are necessary to cause us to grow spiritually as we should. If we have an unbalanced view of the Trinity, it will lead to an unbalanced spirituality.

The communal nature of God is the basis of Christian community. Knowing God, we desire community. Experiencing the Trinity, we begin to treat others differently. We want to recreate the Holy Dance with other believers. God encourages us to break out of our individualistic lives and to build true Christian community.

11
Covenant Relationships

In talking privately with missionaries about their spiritual lives, I have often heard comments such as, "I feel spiritually dry." "Everything seems so dull and routine." "I don't feel the closeness to God I once did." In going deeper in conversation, the comments usually become, "I feel so lonely. I feel cut off from good fellowship." Their feeling of spiritual dryness often traces back to a lack of deep, heart-felt relationships with other believers.

"Psychic isolation" can be a persistent problem for missionaries. We may be surrounded by people, yet not find someone who really understands us. As one missionary said to me, "Back home I was part of a wonderful Christian fellowship of medical professionals but now nothing here equals it and I feel like I'm in a crisis." Many missionaries do make wonderful relationships among the people they serve, but it is not easy to find others who truly understand all that we are and all that we face.

There is the added possibility that we may never have experienced a fulfilling and healing fellowship at all, since so many societies now are superficial and self-sufficient. When we read the New Testament, Christian fellowship was marked by giving, accountability and serving, with such covenantal and mutual activities emphasized such as the "one anothers":

Accepting one another
Agreeing with one another
Being kind to one another
Being hospitable to one another
Bearing one another's burdens

Caring for one another
Encouraging one another
Forgiving one another
Honoring one another
Laying down our lives for one another
Living in harmony with one another
Loving one another
Speaking truthfully to one another
Teaching and admonishing one another

When we have close spiritual friends in our lives — people with whom we can laugh, play, eat, cry and pray together — we immediately see the difference it makes.

Authentic community was very important in the early days of the Protestant missionary movement. Count Nicholas von Zinzendorf (1700-1760), one of the originators of Protestant missions, dedicated himself to a Moravian community that was wracked by division. Due to Zinzendorf's influence, the Moravians achieved true reconciliation by agreeing to live under a covenant and by developing small covenant groups called *banden*. This led to a powerful spiritual renewal during a Communion service on 13 August 1727. From all of these events, which emphasized authentic covenant relationships, the first major Protestant mission movement sprang.

John Wesley (1703-1791), the Methodist evangelist, followed the lead of the Moravians and also organized his converts into small groups that he called "bands" for the purpose of mutual accountability for spiritual growth. Wesley's bands, which focused on intensive, personal accountability and discipleship, had a major impact on English and American societies. It is widely stated that Wesley's work among the poor preserved England from a revolution like the French Revolution.

What are Covenant Relationships?

In covenant relationships we practice covenantal virtues. And so we see Israel, in its covenantal relationship with God, required to walk humbly and to practice mercy and justice toward each other (Micah 6:8). The major virtues in their covenantal life with God were humility, merciful love (*hesed*), faithfulness (*emeth*) and justice (*mishpat*). These same covenantal virtues shaped the Christian community in the New Testament. The Old Testament *hesed*, or "merciful love" became the *agape* love of the New Testament. It is a sacrificial, giving love represented best by Christ, who told us to make *agape* our main virtue:

> *John 13:34-35 A new command I give you: Love one another. As I have loved you, so you must love one another. By this everyone will know that you are my disciples, if you love one another.*

A covenant group is not just another study group or coffee klatch, but a covenanted circle of 2-8 people who agree to walk together. When we enter into that covenant, we seek to go beyond "pseudo-community" to try to create a Christian community marked by the covenantal virtues. The covenant need not be formally written out, but it must be clearly understood: all the members must consider it important and want to live under it.

They agree to share their lives in Christ together. That means they will be humble and open to each other. They will serve one another and give God's grace to one another and show acceptance. As trust builds, they will tell each other the story of their lives. Above all, they will make themselves mutually accountable to each other for their spiritual growth, since their covenant is under God.

It can take time to build a group marked by trust and honest sharing. In the long run, a covenant group will only work if we allow ourselves to be known. We have to be willing to leave pretense aside. When we tell our stories, we will be open to mentioning the sorrows as well as the joys. We will include the failures, temptations and struggles — and not just the triumphs. We will not neglect talking about our human weakness, doubts, fears and true motives. There has to be vulnerability.

In covenant relationships like these, we must also be willing to be confronted and to make ourselves accountable to others. We agree to allow others to pray for us and to speak honest words of counsel and godly admonition. The members of a group may even want to ask each other accountability questions such as: "Have you done, said or seen anything you should not have since we last met?" or, "Do you felt weak and tempted in any area of your life?"

A covenant group is meant to be a redemptive refuge in which we watch over each other. In it, we will do nothing to hurt or reject another. Instead, agape love, "always protects, always trusts, always hopes, always perseveres" (1 Corinthians 13:7). Our desire will be to listen to each other, keep confidences and protect each other.

When we begin covenant relationships with other people, it will change us by making us less independent and more inter-dependent with others. It might even cause us to change our lifestyles as we live for one another. This is also part of becoming more authentic in our relationships with other Christians.

Covenant groups exist to foster an environment for spiritual growth. This happens best when there is shepherding and care-giving, transparency, accountability and intentional spiritual formation. When we practice these things, we grow. When we lack them, we do not grow. We are meant to experience God through each other, not just alone.

Covenant groups take many different forms. The members of each group must decide on their own structure and what spiritual disciplines they wish to practice together. Some groups will study the Bible and pray, others will read Christian authors, or be involved in social justice work. But the heart and soul of a covenant group must always be the sharing of the joys and struggles of being a disciple in Christ. The structure of the group must never squeeze out this regular personal sharing about one's walk with Christ. If it does, the group will cease to be a true covenant group.

The culture of the participants will also affect the form of a covenant group. In egalitarian cultures, people tend to share freely with their peers. In non-egalitarian cultures, there is a tendency to discuss certain subjects only alone with an older, spiritual leader. Again, each group must work out how it will form community and grow in Christ in an honest and accountable way.

We can have a covenant relationship with just one other person or in a covenant group with several other people. Usually, it is best not to have more than 6-8 people in a group since scheduling conflicts will arise, defeating the purpose of the covenant.

Covenant groups are generally closed groups since this is best for fostering trust, openness and spiritual formation. Some covenant groups will last for many years with the same people. However, a covenant group may decide to remake itself from time to time to allow some people to leave who cannot continue and others to join.

Missionaries in isolated areas may have to be creative with their covenant relationships if it is impossible to meet regularly with others. It might be best to have several covenant relationships scattered around to increase the possibility of fellowship. Many missionaries are now using the internet as an option for fellowship with good results, despite its obvious drawbacks. The important thing is to formally agree with one or more people to walk in covenant together with them, and then to work out the details.

Respecting the Spirituality of Others

The Apostle Paul writes:

> **Romans 14:4-5** *Who are you to judge someone else's servant? To their own master, servants stand or fall. And they will stand, for the Lord is able to make them stand. One person considers one day more sacred than another; another considers every day alike. Each of them should be fully convinced in their own mind.*

Whenever our team was training missionaries in spiritual formation, we always included an exercise designed to help everyone learn to respect each other's spirituality. The exercise comes two parts, which we outline below to encourage you to adapt and use in your own groups.

Part One: The "Spirituality and Psychology" Exercise

I once talked with a friend about some spiritual experiences with God that I had been having. At the time I was a young Christian and I thought that all Christians normally had similar experiences. It puzzled me to learn that my friend was different! He was a godly person, but he was also a concrete thinker and could not relate to my mystical bent. I am intuitive and experience God primarily in my inner world. My friend is rooted in his five senses and tends to experience God more through people and situations.

I began to wonder, "Can personality shape spirituality?" Many Christian psychologists would answer, "Yes" to this question.

Some of us are familiar with the Myers-Briggs Type Indicator, or MBTI. It is an attempt to categorize human personalities according to basic types. It was developed by trial and error through decades of research and it offers helpful suggestions for why we prefer some things that others do not. For instance, some people like everything to be orderly and planned, while others thrive when things happen spontaneously. Conflict can develop between people who have two contrasting types of personality.

The MBTI also explains why we prefer some spiritual practices over others. There are people who prefer orderly worship in which the hymns are announced, prayers are read and nothing unusual happens. Others find such a worship service to be meaningless and may even say that it is "dead." They prefer something that is more spontaneous, which they equate to being "spiritually alive."

If personality does influence spirituality, then it is important for us to understand how, so that we can learn to respect each other's walk with God. A beginning would be to take a MBTI test or its equivalent and to have a professional interpret the results. Many organizations now require this testing for new recruits. When a test is taken in a professional setting with a trained specialist who interprets the results, it can be extremely helpful.

In our seminar for missionaries, we were not able to have people take a comprehensive personality test. Instead, we gave a general introduction to the whole subject and asked people to rank themselves *in general* on the eight indicators that Myers-Briggs theory uses to understand human personality. Despite the obvious weaknesses in our approach, it did prove to be a practical means to encourage greater sensitivity.

INTROVERSION-EXTROVERSION (I-E)

The first two indicators in MBTI are *introversion* and *extroversion*. The first question we ask our seminar groups is, "Are you more of an introvert or an extrovert?" For most people, this would be a fairly easy determination to make.

Introversion and extroversion refers to how we orient our personalities. Extroverts orientate themselves around people. They like people, feel energized by them and look forward to being with them. It's a joy, not a chore. Extroverts live in the outer world of people and things.

Introverts orientate themselves around themselves. They like to be alone so they can recharge themselves. They don't really look forward to being with people and may have to push themselves to do so. After introverts are with people, they tend to retreat. They exist in an inner world of concepts and ideas.

Of course, few of us are totally extroverted or introverted. Normally, we lie somewhere on the continuum.

After explaining this, I then distributed the following:

← *More Introverted* (I)   *More Extroverted* (E) →

5— —4— —3— —2— —1— —0— —1— —2— —3— —4— —5

I asked people to choose a number on the scale that best seemed to describe themselves. "Are you a little more on the introverted side? A lot on the extroverted side? Or somewhere right in the middle? Pick a place on the scale."

SENSING- INTUITION (S-N)

The second two categories are *sensing* and *intuition*. This also tends to be an easy determination we can make about ourselves. Sensing and intuition concerns how we perceive the world.

Sensing people tend to perceive the world through their five senses. They are very concrete people, grounded in reality and practical. They like facts and hard data.

Intuitive people perceive the world through their intuition. They live in their own heads. They may daydream, think and imagine. They often rely on hunches to form impressions about what is going on. They can be inventive, and may even be a little unobservant of what is happening around them:

← *More Sensing* (S)   *More iNtuitive* (N) →

5— —4— —3— —2— —1— —**0**— —1— —2— —3— —4— —5

THINKING-FEELING (T-F)

The third set of categories is *thinking* and *feeling*. This concerns how we make decisions.

A thinking person makes decisions through a rational analysis of all the different factors and reasons involved. They like to see things objectively and concisely. They like to know what is right and wrong in a situation.

Feeling people make decisions based on the values that feel right for them in a situation. Sometimes, they can see both sides of an issue. They like to go with their heart rather than their head.

How do you tend to make decisions – by feeling your way through an issue, or by reasoning your way through? Where might you place yourself on the thinking-feeling scale?

← *More Thinking* (T)   *More Feeling* (F) →

5— —4— —3— —2— —1— —**0**— —1— —2— —3— —4— —5

JUDGING-PERCEIVING (J-P)

The last scale concerns how we prefer to live our lives.

"Judging" means we like to live in an orderly world where there are no real surprises: things happen on time and everything is in its place. You wake up in the morning and you very much know what your day will be. You like having a plan and you like when things run according to schedule.

"Perceiving" means that we prefer to live in a more spontaneous world. We like it when someone calls us and interrupts our plans to do something unexpected. We thrive when things are uncertain. We enjoy working with the unknown. We tend to be more scattered and disorganized in our ways. We like to leave our schedule open to respond to changing events.

Jot down where you think you are on the judging-perceiving scale:

← *More Judging* (J)   *More Perceiving (P)*→

5— —4— —3— —2— —1— —**0**— —1— —2— —3— —4— —5

In our seminars, after we asked everyone these questions, we then sought to determine which personality type appeared to be the most dominant within the group as a whole. We did not ask anyone to share the specific numbers by which they scored themselves, since this is just a general exercise. We did ask them to share what side of each scale they felt their personality lay. We then averaged the totals to find the dominant personality type for the group. For instance, a group may find that it tends as a whole toward being ESTJ: Extroverted, Sensory, Thinking and Judging. There are 16 possible combinations of these personality types.

We then had some fun:

1. I asked our seminar participants to discuss what would happen if a new leader came who had a personality that was opposite to that of the group.
2. I asked them to guess which personality type makes the best administrators. (It's ESTJ).
3. Which makes the best teachers? (They tend to be ENFJs since the NF personality component causes teachers to connect with students. ENTJs also reportedly are outstanding teachers, especially in promoting debate and inquiry.)

4.   What type of a person would like to do Ignatian prayer exercises the best. (Those with a "Sensory" S component).

5.   Who would be the natural mystic? (These tend to be INFPs, who like to pursue their spiritual journey alone. INFJ are similar, but they prefer the more structured environment of convents and monasteries.)

6.   I told them that missionary retreat leaders tend to have an INFP or INFJ personality, while mission leaders tend to have the exact opposite personality, ESTJ. We discussed how the exercises used in retreats might be made to appeal to different personality types.

7.   I then asked them, "What do you conclude as a result of what we just did?" Usually, the answers are statements like, "Be aware that others may relate to God differently from you." Or, "develop a walk with God that fits you."

8.   We also talk about the need to challenge ourselves to experience God in new ways that might *not* match our natural personalities. [1]

Part Two: The "Spiritual Traditions" Exercise

In an urban seminary class I once taught, I asked the class to write a review of Philip Yancey's book *The Jesus I Never Knew*. In looking over their reports, I noticed an interesting trend. A student who had been a tough street fighter wrote, "Jesus was so macho." A Latino woman who had been abused wrote, "Jesus was so sensitive to women." An young African-American preacher who was a community champion for human rights wrote, "Jesus was such a revolutionary." An African American matriarch who was married to a bishop wrote, "Jesus was so wise." Each perspective was correct, but everyone saw only themselves and their world in Jesus's personality.

I used that assignment to say to them, "When you teach about Jesus, also teach about those aspects of Jesus that are different from you. Jesus is so much bigger than any one of us: he is all of the above and more."

Richard J. Foster wrote a helpful book in 2001 titled *Streams of Living Water: Celebrating Great Traditions of Christian Faith*. The basic premise of the book is that there are streams of spirituality within Christianity, and that each of these streams reflects different aspects of Jesus. No one stream totally captures who Jesus is. Foster's streams are:

1. The Contemplative Tradition
2. The Holiness Tradition
3. The Charismatic Tradition
4. The Social Justice Tradition
5. The Evangelical Tradition
6. The Incarnational Tradition

Foster explains each of these streams — giving historical, biblical and contemporary examples. He also critiques each tradition, explaining its strengths and weaknesses. He suggests that, if we are to grow in spiritual formation, we have to learn from all these major streams of Christian spirituality because they all reflect who Jesus is. None of our traditions alone perfectly reflects Jesus.

When we read Foster's book, it raises three important questions:

1. With what stream do I most identify?
2. What are the strengths and weaknesses of my stream?
3. What can I learn from the other streams?

This approach to spirituality is helpful because it expands our thinking and helps us to see our own spirituality in a new light. Not only do we feel respected in our own spiritual traditions, but we also feel challenged. Awareness of the various streams teaches balance, encourages respect for all the streams and helps us to avoid the weaknesses of our own spiritual tradition. And it opens us to receive grace from each other.

In our seminar, we did an exercise based on Foster's six traditions. The exercise works best when there are at least 20 people.

First, we reviewed Foster's descriptions of the six different traditions. We then asked everyone to group themselves according to the tradition which influenced them the most. Each subgroup then discussed the strengths and weaknesses of their tradition and reported their answers to the entire larger group. Finally, we compared everyone's answers with Foster's answers in his book.

As you do this exercise, be sensitive to the learning possibilities. For instance, you may find that only a few people have grouped themselves into the "social justice" tradition, or into the "contemplative" tradition. You might ask them, "How does this make you feel?" Explore the implications of belonging to a minority spiritual tradition. Or, if most people in your mission belong to only one tradition, discuss how they can grow by learning from other spiritual traditions.

There is a lot to explore here, so be sure to give yourselves sufficient time to do both exercises mentioned in this chapter: the psychological and the spiritual traditions. I suggest a minimum of 45 minutes for each.

13
Solitude

One night, I was in an ocean resort town where I was conversing with a friend about his life. As we talked, we went on a pier that jutted far into the ocean. Looking back at the town from a distance, we saw it for what it was —a gaudy strip of carnival stores hugging the shore line. There you could throw darts for prizes, or get your face painted. The resort stretched out before us in Vanity Fair makeup as we talked about life and Christ. Somehow just our simple action of withdrawing gave us the perspective we needed to think about eternity.

The cure for worldliness is to see the world for what it really is. Solitude does this for us. When we withdraw, we see. This is why Henri Nouwen said, "Without solitude it is virtually impossible to live a spiritual life." [1] He did not mean that we should constantly go on retreats, but that our souls need to have time with God. Solitude is not being alone. It is being alone with God.

Richard Foster defines solitude as voluntarily abstaining "from our normal patterns of activity and interaction with people for a time in order to discover that our strength and well-being come from God alone." He says that when we first practice solitude, we mostly want to get a break from the world so we can re-enter it again renewed. But then, over time, we discover that solitude actually frees us from the world. We learn to listen to God, rather than to the opinion of others. We begin basing our self-esteem on our relationship with God rather than on what others are saying about us.

Other changes also happen:

Painfully, we let go of the vain images of ourselves in charge of everything and everybody. Slowly, we loosen our grip on all those projects that to us seem so significant. Gently, we become more focused and simplified. Joyfully, we receive the nourishment of heavenly manna. [2]

I served the Coptic Orthodox Christians of Egypt for a number of years. One of their most influential leaders was Kyrillos VI (1902-1971). He was a miracle-worker and a "Mutawahhad" – a Solitary. Before he was chosen to be the leader of his church, Kyrillos spent years living in solitude with God in an abandoned windmill overlooking Old Cairo.

In 1968, he presided over an important ceremony with President Gamel Abd el Nassar of Egypt and Emperor Haile Selassie of Ethiopia. At the end of the day, Kyrillos asked his deacon, "Did you see all these great ceremonies today, my son?" Yes, the deacon had seen everything that day. Kyrillos then said, "All these ceremonies, my son, are not equal to one day spent in the solitude of the windmill above Old Cairo." Kyrillos, practicing contemplative prayer in the ruins of the windmill, felt that he had a richness without equal in this world.

When we meet God in solitude, it develops our relationship with God. It may seem strange, then, to include a chapter on solitude in a broader section on Community, but solitude also renews our love for people. It does this by giving us two gifts for our relationships with others: the gift of compassion and the gift of perspective.

The Gift of Compassion

The Apostle John warns, "Dear children, keep yourselves from idols" (1 John 5:21). He was talking about the things that dull our love for God and people. The world is full of glitzy idols that appeal to us. It is only when we periodically get away from it all that we can see more clearly. In solitude, we come clean and "de-idolize" our hearts.

Thomas Merton (1915-1968) was a monk and a prolific writer. Before he entered into one particular period of solitude, he said how much he despised the world. After he emerged from solitude, he wondered if he would still have the same feelings. Instead, he found that solitude had the opposite effect on him:

> I met the world and I found it no longer so wicked after all. Perhaps the things I had resented about the world when I left it were defects of my own that I had projected upon it. Now, on the contrary, I found that everything stirred me with a deep and mute sense of compassion. [3]

When solitude lessens our attraction for the world's idols, our compassion for others will grow since we become less occupied with ourselves. Solitude increases solidarity.

The Gift of Perspective

Solitude not only gives us the gift of compassion for people, it also gives us the gift of perspective.

Over the long-run, one of the greatest dangers when we serve God is to lose our perspective. The continuing obligations and daily routines, the tyranny of the urgent, the boredom and the monotony of continually serving — these things subtly yet surely change us over time until we forget our vision and true priorities. But when we periodically enter into solitude, it helps us to keep perspective.

When we first start out in mission service, we tend to have the mind of a sprinter who runs with brilliant bursts of energy. With time, we learn that our service is really more of a long-distance run than a sprint.

As much as eighty percent of the running muscles of an Olympic sprinter are "fast-twitch" fibers that are *glucose-burning*, producing quick bursts of energy in a dash. In contrast, as much as eighty percent of the running muscles of an Olympic marathoner are composed of "slow-twitch" fibers — which burn *oxygen* for a slower yet more consistent energy output. If we are to last as mission servants, sooner or later we have to change our thinking from sprinting to long-distance running. When we are sprinting, we simply do not realize how limited our burst of energy will be. When we begin marathoning, we do not realize just how far we can truly run. Indeed, this is why we tend to overestimate what we can accomplish in a year and underestimate what we can get done in five.

The rhythms of solitude, then, are more important than we might realize at first. In fact, when we are thinking like sprinters, solitude seems like a ridiculous interruption — a worthless pause in the race. Perhaps we can begin to understand why the Benedictines went so far as to *plan* their holy pauses to fall every few hours, with bells interrupting urgencies, so they could mingle their being with their doing. Their pauses for prayer were stepping stones through the day to check on their hearts. If you will, they regarded prayer to be the greater urgency for their lives.

I once met a school principal who knew everyone by name — students, parents and staff. He genuinely cared for each of these people. In return, to put it mildly, everyone loved him. I asked him one day, "What's your secret? What makes you like this?" He replied simply, "For the last twenty years, I've been reading the Bible every day. I think that made the difference." Little did he know that he was following his own version of the old Benedictine daily rhythm of work and prayer. In his role as a principal, he was running like a long-distance monk.

Similar to that principal, many missionaries have learned the value of practicing daily solitude. Scripture does9 not dictate to us the exact form this solitude should take, but they do remind us to dwell on God's everlasting presence every day.

On a weekly basis, Sabbaths also deepen perspective within us by rudely interrupting our mundane worlds. Each new Sabbath stands at our door to announce, "Life is not all work." Sabbaths quell our inner compulsions and encourage us to renew our love for God and neighbor. Once a week, when we let the world go on without us, we learn how to play in God's providential care.

Missionaries will sometimes resist keeping a Sabbath out of fear that the practice will become legalistic. But the Sabbath was given to help us find adequate rest and renewal. Sabbath-keeping is one of the more important spiritual disciplines for missionaries who want to run their race for a long time.

Beyond these daily and weekly rhythms of solitude, we can also develop other disciplines of solitude on our own. Some may want to go on a monthly retreat. Others may wish to have a yearly time of reflection before God. There is no rule about it. Each of us finds the patterns of solitude which best suit our own needs and goals.

Single missionaries may also wish to develop rhythms of solitude to gain perspective over loneliness. Marjory F. Foyle, the missionary psychiatrist, encouraged single missionaries to rely on the spiritual discipline of solitude in this way:

> *Loneliness means being alone with yourself, whereas solitude means being alone with God. I mean this literally. Single people often find that the pains of loneliness can be overcome by the knowledge that God is with them in the house. If he is not, then he is not keeping his promise to be with us always. Such experience takes a long time to gain, and there are many pangs of loneliness to be overcome as the knowledge of his permanent presence is developing.* [4]

As we practice solitude periodically, we will gain both the gifts of compassion and perspective, thereby increasing our ability to discern what is truly important in our relationships even as we develop our relationship with God.

Leading in Community

S ometimes, our experience of community involves a power difference over others. When we are in leadership we are in community with others, yet we also have power over them and are influencing them toward a goal. This presents us with special challenges.

Everyone is a Leader

Leaders are everywhere. They include not just the politicians and executives of this world, but any person who makes things happen. A typical mid-sized hospital, for instance, will have over 100 leaders — including all the nurses, physicians and staff who lead the teams that allow a hospital to function.

A leader is anyone who influences others toward a goal. We lead by initiating, organizing, managing, envisioning, guiding, nurturing and mentoring — to name a few of the ways of leading. We may be given an official title, or just rise to leadership in a single situation. Even in a family, we are leaders simply by being parents. In some traditions, a couple is crowned when they are married to symbolize their leadership roles in the world as husband and wife.

Leaders are everywhere, but what is lacking in many leaders is spiritual depth.

Distrust in leadership is an ever-recurrent theme in the news. As I write, an American governor who seriously lied refuses to resign. In Europe, a prime minister is suspected of releasing a terrorist for oil contracts. And in China, a major business scandal has erupted involving an important mining company. Every day carries similar news stories about leaders who have compromised themselves.

Closer to home, we all have our stories of leaders who have disappointed us. It could be a pastor who shattered the trust of a church. Or a colleague who sabotaged a project. We may even be questioning our own role in some difficult situation. One thing is certain: we all want our leaders to be deep people — men and women whom we can respect and trust.

So, when we find ourselves leading others, how can we be good leaders? People have been wondering about that question since the dawn of time, but only since the beginning of the 20th century have we sought to answer it in a scientific way. So, what have we been learning?

Personal Authenticity

One of the things we have been discovering is that spirituality plays an important role in leadership by fostering personal authenticity and integrity. While we cannot explore all the vast research about leadership since 1900, we can quickly trace the growing significance of spirituality.

Formal studies on leadership began around 1900. The earliest studies sought to identify the *personality traits* of good leaders. It was thought that once these traits were known, then anyone who aspires to be a leader could simply emulate these traits to achieve leadership success.

This early research into the common personality traits of leaders ended in failure. In 1948, Ralph Stogdill published a review of all the previous studies and concluded that leaders have such widely varying personalities that no definitive list of traits could be produced. Furthermore, merely imitating a leader proved to be no guarantee of success. Mimicry is not the same as personal authenticity.

After the failure of this early research, the emphasis in the middle of the 20th century shifted away from investigating leadership traits to studying leadership *behaviors.* Researchers sought to answer the question, "What actions of a leader produce the best results?" It was discovered that leaders who care about their team members and not just about goals are more effective since their team becomes more motivated.

Further work built on this by exploring the *relationship* between leader and follower. James M. Burns' book *Leadership* (1978) popularized the concept of the "transformational" leader. It's the leader whose personal qualities inspire team members to transcend their own self-interests for the good of the group. In contrast, "transactional" leaders focus most of their energy on meeting rules, regulations and requirements.

Another seminal book was Robert K. Greenleaf's *Servant Leadership* (1977). Before Greenleaf, we understood leadership as leaders guiding followers. In contrast, Greenleaf's thinking led to the development of the leader-team model in which a leader is conceived as a "first among equals."

Because of Greenleaf's focus on relationships and personal genuineness, leadership studies began exploring the interior life of leaders. By the mid-1990's, researchers began studying the *spirituality* of leaders. Keep in mind that sociological researchers use the word "spirituality" to refer to a person's inner integrity and authenticity.

Utilizing the methods of sociological research, studies quickly produced interesting results. In particular, they vindicated such traditional spiritual virtues as integrity, honesty and humility. In 2005, Laura Reave concluded in her cross-study of 150 reports:

All of the following practices have ... been found to be crucial leadership skills: showing respect for others, demonstrating fair treatment, expressing caring and concern, listening responsively, recognizing the contributions of others, and engaging in reflective practice.

Her findings also refute the Machiavellian type of leader:

Many experts expect strategy, intelligence, even ruthlessness to be marks of a successful leader. ... Instead, spiritual values such as integrity, honesty, and humility have been repeatedly found to be key elements of leadership success. [1]

As we look back over these sociological leadership studies, there has been a gradual shift from just identifying the external traits and behaviors of a leader to understanding the crucial role that inner authenticity plays in leadership. Increasingly, we have been learning how spirituality makes good leaders by fostering this authenticity through the development of traditional spiritual virtues.

Personal Identity

If we are to lead others in a godly way, we must not only be authentic by developing traditional spiritual virtues, but we also need to have a healthy personal identity.

Leadership brings us many pressures that can easily warp our sense of self-identity. We may begin defining ourselves by what we do, the power we possess or the title we have. When we see our name towards the top of an organizational chart, we may start thinking that we are better than others. In many organizations, our power over others is often reinforced by salary differences, thereby structurally reinforcing our feelings of self-importance.

There are several things that we can do to combat these distortions in our self-identity.

First, we may wish to take to heart the teaching of the Desert Fathers that self-importance is one of the more dangerous sins. Evagrious the Solitary advises to drive away the demon, "by intense prayer and by not doing or saying anything that contributes to the sense of your own importance."[2] At all costs, we are to avoid using our position to feed our egos.

Secondly, a mission might actually consider equalizing the salaries of all its workers, from the newest recruit to the mission executives. This was the practice in our mission and it effectively promoted the idea that everyone has a significant role.

Thirdly, we can rebuild our sense of identity around God by reading the Bible while asking the question, "What does this passage teach me about my true identity before God?" For instance, Psalm 139 tells us that we are "fearfully and wonderfully made," and that God's thoughts for us "outnumber the grains of sand." Romans 5:1 tells us that "we have peace with God through our Lord Jesus Christ." And Romans 8:15 informs us that we are God's children. This is a way of reminding ourselves that our real identity is in God.

Fourthly, within Protestant spirituality there is also the useful concept of the "two callings" — our primary and our secondary callings. Our primary calling is to live for God. Our secondary calling is what we do for a living.

Our primary calling to be a disciple always take priority over any role or job we may have. Our careers are important, but who we are as people before God is even more important. That means we should work hard toward our career objectives, but we must always keep everything in perspective. Our primary calling is to mature our souls for God. Our secondary calling is to perform our role in this world to contribute to society.

When we keep this in mind, it preserves us from developing bloated identities. When our primary calling is in order, it gives us a greater ability to handle setbacks, respect the importance of others and graciously leave our positions of leadership when the time eventually comes.

Leadership Styles within Missions

For those of us who are called to leadership within a mission, we should realize that the style of leadership in missions has been changing over the decades from a heroic style to more of a collegial style. It is important to understand these two styles of mission leadership as well as their strengths and weaknesses.

Heroic Leadership

Jesus was a heroic leader. He was willing to go against the crowd, live a life of endurance for others and to suffer personally. It says that Jesus "endured the cross, scorning its shame" (Hebrews 12:2). Similarly, our Lord tells us to be willing to deny ourselves, take up our crosses and follow him (Mark 8:34).

In the past, many mission executives practiced a heroic style of leadership. In his classic book, *Spiritual Leadership*, J. Oswald Sanders portrays leaders almost exclusively as individualistic heroes. True to his time, he never depicts mission leaders as being part of a collegium.

In fact, Sanders says that leaders are *meant* to be lonely:

From its very nature, the lot of the leader must be a lonely one. He must always be ahead of his followers. ... In his journey to the top he had left behind all his contemporaries and stood alone in the mount with his God. ... It is often heartbreaking to have to make decisions of far-reaching importance which affect the lives of loved fellow workers — and to make them alone. [3]

Such a style of leadership is attractive to those who come from cultures that glorify the heroic leader, but it does have its problems. It is highly individualistic and can cause a leader to over-function, micro-manage and to create dependencies. It can make us feel that we are indispensable and that we must be chronically fatigued to be virtuous. It can also foster burn-out and family problems.

There will always a place for hard work and sacrifice, but the problems inherent with heroic leadership has encouraged a welcomed shift within mission organizations toward a more collegial style.

Collegial Leadership

Jesus also was also a collegial leader. He developed his leadership team around three men whom he knew personally and who knew each other well. Two of them were Jesus' first cousins — James and John. Their mother was Salome, Mary's sister (cf. Matthew 27:56, Mark 16:1, John 19:25). James and John were in business with Peter (Luke 5:10). Jesus was so close to these three men that he gave them all nicknames. He called Peter, "*Rocky*," and James and John, the "*Sons of Thunder*" —cousins have been called a lot worse!

These men became Jesus' closest confidants. At times, we read how he gave exclusive access only to them, with John the closest to Jesus of all (Luke 8:51, 9:28). Jesus knew that leadership depends on relationships. He was personal friends with his leadership team, but he also knew when to act with authority toward them.

Jesus did not call his apostles to be lonely. He called them to have relationships with other apostles. He sent them out in pairs, which was a deliberate attempt to provide encouragement and accountability. Jesus expected his apostolic leaders to care about their fellow apostles instead of acting solely as individuals.

As a result, when the apostles founded churches, they adopted the same collegial model of leadership they learned from Christ. The apostles made decisions together (Acts 2:42-47; 15:1-29). They taught that a church is the "body of Christ" in which all the members are important and bear responsibility for each other (Romans 12:3-8, 1 Corinthians 12). They also ordained elders and deacons to serve together as colleagues in churches.

Despite all this, collegial leadership also has its problems. For instance, the leadership team in a mission can degenerate into a group of insipid chumps who hesitate to take any initiative on their own or who shy from debating anything vigorously less it impair the nice atmosphere.

Since Christ exemplifies both collegial and hero leadership, the ideal of Christian leadership must include both. We are meant to be strong, sacrificial leaders who also can work together as a team. Such an ideal way of functioning takes time to develop yet is a healthier form of leadership that Jesus himself exemplifies.

Part Three: Ministry

15

Incarnational Ministry

"Ministry is not just an activity, but it is a spirit transferred from one person to another. It is a life which the person ministered to absorbs from the one who serves." (Shenouda III, leader of the Coptic Orthodox Church in Egypt)

In Christian service, who we are is as important as what we do. Some of our most important work as missionaries will be to embody God's care and compassion to people in need. We call this *incarnational ministry.*

Despite the importance of incarnational ministry, we usually receive little training in it. This is because it is not an academic subject that can be tested and graded, but rather it is the byproduct of our own spiritual formation. Nonetheless, certain Christian professions, especially chaplains, have thought long and hard about incarnational ministry.

In this chapter I will outline the training necessary to conduct an incarnational ministry as a chaplain in an acute care facility. The concepts are adaptable to other types of incarnational ministry as well, so each individual will have to think through what is important for their situation. It should be said that this is just an outline; formation training is far easier to summarize than to implement.

It's Being, not just Doing

Missionaries are doers. We're trained to serve and to help. Yet, incarnational ministry requires us to learn to be, not just to do. *Being is a much harder lesson to learn.*

When a trained chaplain enters a hospital room, his or her main concern should not be on doing anything. We may find ourselves helping a patient with a pillow, or getting a nurse, but mostly we are there just as a friend who listens and cares. We do not try to solve unsolvable problems, but instead we accept people non-judgmentally, stay with them in their crisis, encourage them and bless any step they take toward God and wholeness. We try to embody the care and compassion of Christ.

Our natural urge is to do something. We feel this urge because we want to help, or to solve problems, or to relieve our own anxiety and nervousness. We do not realize that our desire to do something is actually our attempt to control the situation.

Many situations — especially the worse ones — cannot be controlled. Or solved. Or helped. They just are. And they require us just to be. In that being — in our relationship with the person we are serving— we have to trust the presence of Christ to minister through us.

When we begin a ministry of "being," we find ourselves constantly getting in the way. We steer conversations to suit our own interests. We visit to serve our own needs. We arrive with our own anxieties, fears and prejudices that prevent Christ from working through us. We are still trying to control the situation instead of allowing the God who is present within us to work through us.

Before we can do an incarnational ministry, we have to understand what is going on inside ourselves so we can quiet it all down. There are five important lessons to be learned:

1. If we don't understand ourselves, we will continually see ourselves in others.

2. When we accept our own individuality, we will learn to accept the individuality of others.

3. When we accept our own humanness, we will learn to accept the humanness of others.

4. When we understand our own prejudices, we will learn to be non-judgmental.

5. When we are honest about our lack of wholeness, we help people to open up.

I remember serving Holy Communion to one particular patient. During my visit, she told me a horrendous story of her past and then she also acted in an inappropriate manner. I thought it best to stay away in the future.

Two years later, she was back and I had to minister to her again. I really did not want to do it, but she was in distress. In my visits, I saw a different side to her. She had been abused, this was true, but she also suffered from a disorientating mental illness. During my visits, she returned to God and even had visions from God that comforted her. A year later, it was her time to die and I helped her through her last moments and blessed her at death. She experienced God's redemption, love and hope through my incarnational ministry, but first I had to deal with my own prejudices.

Genuinely Welcoming People

In order for people to sense Christ in us, we must learn to genuinely welcome them. This involves far more than simply giving them a warm greeting when we see them.

Greetings, of course, are important. How we greet someone indicates how much we accept them. So, in culturally appropriate ways, we should make eye contact, smile, say warm words and show attentiveness. These basic interpersonal skills of greeting are essential in any incarnational ministry.

But besides just giving people a warm greeting, we also need to go further in order to truly welcome people.

We begin with our own state of mind. If we lack personal serenity, or are embroiled with our own issues, we cannot be a welcoming person. It's a general rule that the more stressed we feel, the less empathetic we will be toward others. To be genuinely attentive to others, we first have to set aside our pre-occupations and distractions. In this way, Jesus set aside his grief for the slain John the Baptist to allow himself to feel compassion for people (Matthew 14:14). Sometimes we are so busy and distracted that we do not want to be interrupted, but then we remember that Providence often works through the interruptions. An incarnational ministry sees interruptions as opportunities.

Likewise, when we judge people, even subtly, they will not feel welcomed by us and we will be unable to have an incarnational ministry. We must be totally convinced that God loves the person who is standing before us. Jesus told us that it is not our place to judge (Matthew 7:1). It is our place to love.

In my hospital work, it took me a long time to learn to accept people in this way. My deepest prejudices were against dysfunctional families and inner city gangs. I remember watching fistfights and people hitting walls and threatening bodily injury to each other. One day I had to deal with a near riot of fifty people who were emotional and irrational. And it was my job to bring the incarnational presence of Christ into these situations. Yet, by not judging, I often was able to bring emotional people into the presence of Christ and prayer.

Love is the main basis for an incarnational ministry. Unless we love people, we will not be able to serve them and unless they love us, they will not get anything from us. When we judge people, we make it harder for God to work through us. To stop judging others, we first have to identify our own prejudices and then consciously set them aside.

But welcoming people into our lives involves even more than just learning not to judge them. It also involves treating other people as our equals. When we think that we are superior to others in any way — perhaps by being more educated or having what we consider to be "better manners" — it hinders our incarnational presence. We have to see significance in every person. As Jesus taught us, "Whatever you did for one of the least of these brothers and sisters of mine, you did for me" (Matthew 25:40).

Scripture teaches that every person is made in the image of God. Although this image is tarnished, it is still the image of God and must be respected (Genesis 9:6). This image can only be fully restored in Christ, who is the perfect image of God (Colossians 1:15), but there is enough of this residual image in every person for us to respect it.

This is why Catholic and Orthodox missionaries will often talk about "seeing Christ" in every person. They are not saying that everyone is a Christian. What they are doing is respecting the image of God in every person. They feel that this emphasis helps them to treat all people with dignity and respect.

In contrast, our evangelical Protestant emphasis has been on "being Christ" to people. Both emphases are needed: to respect the residual image of God in all people and to introduce Christ to people, who can restore the image of God within all of us.

Being with the People We Serve

To have an incarnational ministry we have to want to be with the people we serve. We have to learn to accept people for what they are able to bring to the relationship. Not everyone is interesting or fascinating. Some people will be irritable and difficult. But once we learn to welcome people into our lives without judgment and with respect, we will learn to like them for who they are.

One person I visited could only drool and mutter a few words. I had to learn to accept his drools and willingly wipe his face. Although he struggled with dementia, he nodded every time when I offered him Holy Communion even as God seemed to touch his heart. When his time to die came, his wife told me afterwards what happened. "At the moment he died," she said, "I suddenly saw a man with a robe appear right beside him and I then heard the words, 'Armand, it's time for you to come now.' And he was gone, just like that."

When we serve in an incarnational ministry, we have to ask ourselves, "Am I here for myself or am I here for the person before me?" If we serving for our own purposes, we will not associate with the less interesting and the droolers. But if we have truly come to serve, we will be able to give Christ's love and care to all.

Eventually, after doing this kind of work for a long time, we learn the most important lesson of all in incarnational ministry, and that is that we always receive far more than we give. This lesson comes only after we learn to truly welcome people into our lives and learn to be with them. We become grateful for each person and we look forward to the next opportunity to serve. This is what sustains us over the long haul.

Listening Empathetically

A very important component in the incarnational ministry of a chaplain is empathetic listening. It is listening non-judgmentally and compassionately to the feelings of another.

Empathetic listening, also known as empathic listening, has been described as the "highest form of listening." Most of the time we ignore people or we listen selectively to their words. This is the lowest form of listening!

A higher form of listening is to listen to the words of others, but only from our own perspectives. This causes us to evaluate what others are saying in terms of what we already know. In our replies to people, we tend to give our advice too freely.

We seldom experience or practice empathetic listening. When we do so, we are listening both to *the words and the feelings* of another person compassionately and without judgment. This makes them feel understood, loved and supported. We encourage them to tell us their story by helping them to feel safe. Empathetic listening is one of the greatest acts of love we can do for another person.

When we practice empathetic listening as a servant of Christ, God often works through it. At the end of empathetic listening, I will often ask permission from the other person to say a prayer (but I will do this only if it seems appropriate). During that prayer, people often open up to God with tears.

I remember being asked to visit an alcoholic who said that he was "angry at God." I listened to him empathetically and as I did, he told me of his dying fiancée and started to cry. I continued to listen and to care for him and he opened his heart to God during our time of prayer because someone had listened to his feelings. I also remember another man who had been a soldier in Vietnam. He was a violent and difficult person who was easy to dislike. But as I listened to his story with respect and acceptance, I then offered to pray with him. During the prayer, he cried and afterwards told me that no one had ever listened to him before.

So, how do we do empathetic listening? To be honest, it is a skill that is best learned in a mentored relationship. It is also true that some of the best empathetic listeners are intuitive introverts since people with those personality types are generally more capable of sensing the feelings of others. Besides all this, I will say a few things.

Begin by being as present in your heart and your mind as possible to the other person. Truly welcome and want to be with that person, as I described earlier in this chapter.

As you listen to the person, pay attention to any emotive words or feeling words they may use. When we show care to a person who uses such words, it gives them permission to talk further about their feelings, if they want. Never pry or probe to satisfy your own curiosity. You are there only to be a listening servant to another person, not for your own interests.

Since many people never have anyone in their lives who cares enough to listen to their feelings, their emotions may start gushing out like water from behind an opened dam. When we listen empathetically to them, we are showing Christ's love to them by helping them release all that pent-up water.

Understand that empathetic listening is intensive work and tiring. If you do it well, usually it will make you feel drained and you will need to take some time afterwards to recharge.

Trusting God to Work

When we conduct an incarnational ministry, we must trust and expect that God will work through us. We are not just listening and smiling. We are also expecting and praying for God to work through us. Regular intercessory prayer should be an important part of any incarnational ministry.

I remember visiting a man who politely welcomed me but quickly identified himself as "an atheist and an engineer." He told me, "Thank you for visiting, chaplain, but I don't believe in God." Because he was a welcoming person, however, he wanted me to continue to visit him as a friend. And so I did so, even as I prayed for him in my private prayers.

A few weeks later, he was dying. Shortly before he died, one day he said to me, "God bless you!" I thought, "Now that's odd for an atheist to say." However, around that time, as he related to his family, he said he had a vision in which, "I saw Jesus come and stand right next to my bed." He died having peace with God. He never went to church. He never gave any money to God's work. For almost all his life, he was an atheist. Yet, God had mercy on him. We should do our work of incarnational ministry with the expectation that God will work through us.

The living God is working constantly in the world around us, despite what we may be feeling inside or how people may be reacting to us. We should expect God to work through us.

16

Values and Ethics

W hat a name — Nabal. It means "fool." We find his story in 1 Samuel 25, where we learn that he owned an agri-business consisting of a thousand goats and three thousand sheep. By the way, his family name — Caleb — was no better. It means "dog."

The biblical story tells how David and his men protected "Fool Dog" and his flocks from predatory animals and thieves. When feast time came, David expected a gratuity for his services, but Fool Dog would have none of it. Instead, he gave David a generous insult.

David responded like any Bedouin warrior would. With his honor at stake in front of all his men, and consumed by anger, he marches his men to teach Fool Dog a lesson. Along the way, Abigail, Nabal's wife, meets David before the blood flowed.

She admits that her husband is just like his name, a fool, but then she craftily says that whoever murders a fool becomes one in turn. She reminds David of his life's mission – one day he was meant to be king. Does the future king want needless bloodshed on his conscience? Why should David kill others wantonly when God promises to protect him? Abigail appeals to David's spiritual values which he had forgotten in the heat of the conflict.

David's response was to bless her for "good judgment and for keeping me ... from avenging myself" (1 Samuel 25:33). Yes, it was honorable for him to kill Nabal, but it was neither godly nor wise. Whose values would he live by? What was his real mission anyways? Abigail not only understood who David really was, she also had the courage to tell him of this.

Values-Based Decision-Making

As mission servants, we operate in a world filled with our own Fool Dogs and desert conflicts. In the heat of a moment, we may be tempted to forget the values we live by. While ordinary decisions might be done in default mode, that is not good enough for important matters that affect people for a long time. Those decisions have to be done carefully and according to principle. We cannot simply react to situations with knee-jerk, emotional choices.

In the story of David and Abigail, she forced David into what we would call a values-based decision-making process. She purposely caused David to think through his values while he deliberated over Fool Dog's fate. It is always helpful to have an Abigail or two in any organization. But we can also follow an "Abigail Process."

The Abigail Process begins when an organization clearly understands its own mission and values. This takes time to discern. The development of a clear mission statement and the delineation of an organization's values involves a process of discussion, feedback, education and vision-casting. The process is well-worth it, though, because once people know who they are, they find it easier to figure out what they want when important decisions have to be made in the heat of a situation. Below is a simplified version of a values-based decision-making process:

THE "ABIGAIL PROCESS"

DEFINE *The Abigail process begins when an organization first defines its mission and core values before any specific issue arises.*

DISCERN *An issue arises. The team discerns the values at play behind the issue and compares them with their core values.*

CREATE   The team thinks creatively about the options that best support its organization's values in the light of the situation.

IMPLEMENT   The team implements its best option and evaluates the situation again in a future review.

Making Ethical Decisions

We can follow an Abigail Process for heat-of-the-moment decisions. But sometimes we also need to do deeper ethical thinking, especially when we are in a position of leadership.

Since leadership involves the use of power to influence others toward a goal, ethical problems in leadership often arise over how we use our power. Whether we know it or not, our decisions can affect the lives of people unjustly and unfairly.

For instance, an organization may be struggling to survive in tough economic times. As a missionary leader involved with that organization, you want to develop a plan that will enable it to survive yet you also want to be as fair and just as possible to the personnel involved. You are facing an ethical issue, not because you abused anyone, but because you know that your choices will affect lives.

As mission servants, we want to do the right thing, but this can be very difficult to discern at times. People often rely on a single theory of ethics to guide their choices in a situation, but each theory is limited.

Some, for instance, consider the "ethical thing" to be whatever does **the greatest good** for society as a whole. But we do not always know in advance what the greatest good will be in the long run. It is also possible that our sense of the "greatest good" will be horribly warped, as when the Nazis in World War II thought the greatest good to be the extermination of the Jewish race.

Another approach in ethics has been to do **the most correct thing,** whatever the cost. But ethical dilemmas are shrouded by confusing and conflicting views, making it difficult for us always to know the correct thing to do. Not only that, but we can have a very twisted sense of what is correct, just as we can have for what is the greatest good.

Some then say that we should do *the most loving thing,* whatever the cost. But, again, people have disagreed about what is the most loving thing to do. Is spanking a child a loving act or a crime? Is capital punishment beneficial or barbaric? Is going to war to defend a homeland a loving thing to do? People have their differing views.

Other people base their sense of ethics on *the most just thing* to do. But when this theory is applied to the political realm and economic redistribution is sought, it raises the question whether it penalizes effort and thereby causes society to be *less* productive and just.

Still another ethical approach has been to do *the most responsible thing* for society as a whole. But who determines the most responsible behavior in a community?

In many countries, *the most honorable thing* is considered to be the most ethical. Honor can be a great motivator for sacrifice but it, too, can lead to such a bizarre action as a father who kills his daughter for violating the family honor with a young man. The values which determine the most honorable thing vary among cultures.

Many base their sense of ethics on whatever is *the most loyal thing* to do toward a leader or a group. In this situation, truth is determined by what is best for the group. But this can lead to problems such as adopting unquestioning obedience to a leader who does evil.

Still other people base their sense of right and wrong on what is *most profitable* for their lives, or *most pleasurable*, or the *least troublesome*. But these are certainly self-centered notions of ethics.

No matter what approach we use, we quickly realize that there are limitations and that it is not always easy to determine the most ethical thing to do. At best, we can use all the approaches together to think through an issue from different angles in the hope of making the most informed decision.

When a leadership team must make a decision involving a difficult ethical choice, it must understand the issue as broadly as possible. The team members would follow a values-based decision-making approach, but then ask further questions to widen their understanding. They might, for instance, ask:

Who will be affected negatively by our decision?

Can we foresee any of the long-term consequences?

In this decision, are we simply being loyal to our organization or are we truly making an ethical choice?

Are we able to explain our reasoning and motives to the world?

Will we be comfortable with our decision years from now?

What cultural issues do we need to consider?

A serious problem in leadership teams — one that can undermine ethical decision-making —is *"groupthink."* This is when the members of a team feel the need to be agreeable toward each other more than to truly resolve a problem. When this happens, everyone tends to adopt a single point of view to be nice to each other or because they feel pressured to agree. Communication breaks down as people hide their real opinions. Facts go unchecked or ignored. The result can be fatal.

Leaders can discourage *groupthink* by encouraging free and open discussions and debate and by soliciting contrary views without penalty. People can be taught to be tough, loyal and respectful of each other.

The Value of an Ethical Standard

Mission servants can foster the ethical climate of an organization not only through the ethical decision process, but also by promoting ethical standards. When the 20th century Christian leader Billy Graham first came into prominence, he and his team developed an ethical code to follow. It read:

We will never criticize, condemn, or speak negatively about others.

We will be accountable, particularly in handling finances, with integrity according to the highest business standards.

We will tell the truth and be thoroughly honest, especially in reporting statistics.

We will be exemplary in morals — clear, clean and careful to avoid the very appearance of any impropriety.

Graham's standards set a tone that they influenced many leaders in other Christian organizations as well.

Many businesses and organizations have developed their own ethical codes of conduct, but these codes are only as good as the leaders who enforce them. There is a difference between paper standards and true operating norms. A company that says it does not participate in corruption may quietly do so to keep a contract. It is the leader who must insist on what the ethical standards will be during times of choice.

Bribery and Corruption

It is especially difficult to know what to do as missionaries when we are in places where bribery and corruption are systemic. We may begin thinking, "Corruption is the norm. I must fit in with the system." We may also realize that many workers are underpaid and depend on gratuities to survive.

On the other hand, we may also realize that many practices of bribery are truly corrupt and harmful and even those living in that society wish it could all end. We may find that people may be more open than we realize to organizations which adhere to a higher standard. Christian leaders can lead the way in modeling these standards. Our goal is not simply to get things done, but to get them done in a way that transforms culture.

Still, it takes a great deal of discernment to respond in the right way to situations in which gifts are expected. It is helpful to distinguish between gifts which manipulate and gifts which express gratitude without manipulation. The former corrupts a society, while the later may just help an underpaid worker to survive. And certainly, gifts are never to be received or given to influence a judge in a court of law.

In trying to decide the right thing to do, we can ask ourselves such questions as:

"Have I prayed for God's help and wisdom?"

"If the government or the press knew about this gift, would it be called corruption?"

"Will the gift compromise my Christian witness in the long-term, even if it gets things done for me in the short-term?"

"Am I trying to manipulate, or am I expressing gratitude without any further expectations?"

"Is this gift being used to influence a verdict or a judge?"

Ethics in Multi-cultural Situations

The word "culture" refers to the shared history, attitudes, values, perspectives and practices that characterize a people. Because of these differences, conflicts and misunderstandings can easily erupt in multi-cultural settings.

Years ago, I taught a class in a country not my own. No matter what I said, one person always strongly opposed me. At the time, I felt he was just being ill-tempered. Years later, however, another person from his country spoke candidly to me about the colonialism which caused many from their generation to feel inferior around foreign teachers. He said the oppositional behavior I experienced was due to this.

When a multi-cultural team works through an ethical issue, everyone comes to the table with their own residual backgrounds. The members must learn to talk on a heart-level about their differing values and motives. The team must recognize, for instance, that cultures often have prevailing theories of ethics just as individual people do. One nationality may be very concerned with individual justice and equality, but another nationality might be more concerned with group loyalty. Each culture will have its own sense of right and wrong.

Decision-making on such a team requires a broadening of perspectives until the values of each culture are properly respected. Only then can a decision be achieved that is sensitive to the situation. Decisions based solely on the preferences of one cultural group are counter-productive.

The Ultimate Goal

People tend to base their sense of what is ethical on the goals they desire to achieve. They may be seeking the greatest good, or the most correct thing to do, or the most loving thing. They could also be seeking to determine what is the most just choice in a situation, or the most responsible, or the most honorable or the most loyal thing.

Ultimately, from a Christian perspective, our ethical decision-making is a process of trying to determine the *most pleasing thing to God*. Only God is completely holy and just and good. Our role is to determine, to the best of our abilities, what is right in God's eyes.

We do this by using the various theories of ethics to examine an issue from different perspectives. But, as Christians, we also have the help of the Holy Spirit. When faced with a difficult ethical decision, many leaders quietly pray for wisdom and discernment. In the next chapter we will learn more about understanding the mind of God in the complicated situations we face.

17

Decision-Making and Guidance

S cripture appears to indicate two forms of decision-making and divine guidance. First, there is direct guidance from the Holy Spirit, such as through visions, dreams and an inner sense of compulsion from God. Secondly, there is discerning the will of God by practicing godly wisdom. In this latter possibility, God allows us to make many discretionary decisions on our own. In this chapter, we will discuss both of these possibilities in turn.

Direct Guidance from the Holy Spirit

In Scripture, we read how the Spirit provides specific guidance and even geographical leading. Luke 4:1 tells us that Jesus "was led by the Spirit in the desert." Similarly, Acts 8:39 tells us how the "Spirit of the Lord suddenly took Philip away," and Acts 16:7 mentions that the "Spirit of Jesus would not allow" Paul and his companions to enter Bithynia. This specific guidance happened at God's initiative and to fulfill God's Master Plan.

Such guidance is possible, but we can hardly expect the Spirit to lead us for every matter we pray about. People will sometimes misinterpret several verses to say otherwise. Let's take a look ...

Two major passages that mention the leading of the Spirit are Romans 8 and Galatians 5. There, however, the context relates the leading of the Spirit to our daily behavior and not to specific guidance. These verses describe how the Spirit leads us to live a godly life by convicting us of sin and compelling us to develop the fruit of the Spirit: love, joy, peace, patience, kindness, goodness, faithfulness, gentleness and self-control (Galatians 5:18-25).

Some people also look to certain Psalms to suggest that we can always expect to receive specific guidance through divine leading:

Psalm 25:4,9 *Show me your ways, O Lord, teach me your paths; guide me in your truth and teach me. ... He guides the humble in what is right and teaches them his way.*

Psalm 32:8 *I will instruct you and teach you in the way you should go; I will counsel you and watch over you. (Psalm 32:8)*

But these verses are not promising that God will supernaturally tell us what to do in all situations. Instead, they are promising that God guides us as we study God's ways in God's Word. In these verses, "ways" and "paths" are metaphors for the demands of God's covenant as found in the Law of Moses (see Psalm 25:10, Deuteronomy 8:6).

Some also refer to John 14:26, which reminds us that the Spirit "will teach you all things and will remind you of everything I have said to you." But this is not a promise of guidance, only that the Spirit would help the Apostles to recall Jesus' teachings and its significance.

So, the biblical evidence is that we may experience the specific guidance of the Spirit, but no verse promises this to us on demand. We should certainly pray for providential guidance, but if an answer does not come within a reasonable time, God may be giving the matter over to us to decide.

This caveat aside, many missionaries do report times when they received direct guidance from God. I remember one old missionary, who had served in China before the rise of Communism, tell me personally how God audibly spoke to her to guide her on several occasions. More commonly, we hear God speaking inaudibly within our hearts or prompting us within our souls in some way.

The theologian, Simon Chan, writes about these promptings. Perhaps you have experienced what Simon Chan writes about:

Christians do experience, more often than they realize, moments when they 'feel led' to do something. The name of a person whom we have not seen for some time suddenly comes to mind. We feel an urge to ring up someone. Occasionally something like a burden descends on us, and we just feel a need to pray. ...

Incidents like these happen frequently. We can respond in one of the following ways: (1) ignore the promptings, (2) follow through on every one of them (which over-scrupulous Christians often do) and end up exhausting and confusing ourselves or (3) learn to discern the genuine workings of grace. [1]

Does God Have a Perfect Plan for Us?

When we talk about direct guidance from the Holy Spirit, we must settle in our minds whether or not God has a "perfect plan" for our lives. If we say that he does, then we will expect God to tell us explicitly what to do in all the critical situations we face.

One school of thought says that God does have a perfect plan for everyone, which we must then discover. If we receive no specific guidance, then we are to take no new action until we do so.

Another school says that God does not have a perfect plan for everyone. We can pray for providential guidance, and it may come, but if it does not, we are free to make our own choices using our own godly wisdom.

Certainly, God is capable of giving us providential guidance. The question here is whether we always should expect this to happen according to a perfect plan for each of our lives and organizations.

Let's assume, for the sake of argument, that God does, indeed, have a detailed blueprint for each of our lives. What are the implications?

Let's say that I have married a woman named Jeanne, but it wasn't in God's perfect plan for me to do so. Maybe it was God's perfect plan for me to marry Mei, yet I did not. Logically, that means I am now out of God's perfect plan for my life and Jeanne is my second-best wife. God might bless our marriage, but not as much as if I had I married Mei, as God really had intended.

Let's also say that, according to God's perfect plan, I was supposed to meet Mei the day after I married Jeanne. We never met as God intended because Jeanne and I were on our honeymoon. Mei is now not in God's perfect will, even though she never even met me. It does not really matter — she still is not in God's perfect will. Poor Mei.

Mei ended up marrying Tomas. That means both of them are now not in God's perfect plan because Mei was supposed to marry me. If Tomas marries Mei, then he is not able to marry the person he was supposed to marry according to "The Plan." Through no fault of their own, they're all out of God's perfect plan — all because of me!

And it just goes on like that. Because I did not marry Mei as God intended, then the entire human race will eventually fall out of God's perfect plan. One little mistake and I have destroyed humanity.

It appears that God does not have a rigid, perfect plan for each of us. When we say that there is a detailed life-plan for each of our lives, we actually are believing in fatalism and we are saying that we have a deterministic God.

God is not like that. And this is why the Bible never promises us that we can have specific guidance from God on demand. We experience God's providential care every day. And we also may receive direct guidance on occasion, but this does not imply this must always happen.

God's Master Plan

The Bible never teaches that there is a detailed blueprint for each of our lives, but it does teach that God has a Master Plan for the salvation of the world, a plan that culminates in Christ (Ephesians

3:7-11). When we come to Christ, we become a part of this Master Plan. We may even experience God's providential guidance according to the purposes of this Master Plan.

Other than that, we should recognize that God's providential care for us also allows us to have considerable freedom in the choices we make. It is this way because God wants us to be mature and responsible. We are made in the image of God and have been endowed by our Creator with considerable freedom. Our lives with God are adventures in which we actually get to make many of the choices on the journey.

So, when Paul talks about a woman seeking marriage, he writes: "She is free to marry anyone she wishes, but he must belong to the Lord" (1 Corinthians 7:39). The choice entirely belongs to her, so long as she chooses a believer. If she is free to choose which believer to marry — a most important decision — then certainly we also must be free to make many of our choices in life, as long as we conform to God's moral will. If God wishes to redirect us in our choice, he is capable of doing so.

Making Wise and Godly Decisions

This leads us to consider the second way by which we discern God's will: by making wise and godly decisions.

The people of God in the Bible made godly decisions by studying God's ways and his character. This contrasts noticeably with the practices of pagan nations in ancient history. The records of ancient Assyria and Babylon are filled with accounts of divination — attempts to obtain specific guidance from the gods through such methods as examining the quivering of a freshly-killed liver. There is a world of difference between examining a liver in a bowl and reading Scripture.

Scripture informs us how to make wise and godly decisions by teaching us what is ethical. We are to do such things as to tell the truth, respect property rights and honor marriage. Scripture also teaches us such principles of justice as:

- punishment should not be excessive
- land inheritance is to be secure
- the poor are not to be oppressed
- respect is to be shown to foreigners
- no one is above the law, not even the king
- compassion is to be shown to animals
- all in society are to rest regularly

Furthermore, Scripture also teaches us plainly about God's character so we can know what pleases him. In Exodus 34:6-7, for instance, we learn that God is "compassionate and gracious." This teaches us to act in a similar way toward each other. Likewise, we learn to be just because God requires it: "And what does the LORD require of you? To act justly and to love mercy and to walk humbly with your God" (Micah 6:8).

The Bible is not a comprehensive casebook which tells us in detail what to do in every particular situation. Instead, it teaches us what God is like so that we can decide what pleases God the most. When we read about God's words and ways, we gain insight into God's will for the various situations we face.

Years ago, a fellow missionary asked me, "Should I wait on God to show me what to do next, or should I go ahead and make my wisest choice?" He was a godly man who relied on prayer, but he was wondering about specific guidance.

We talked about Ecclesiastes 9:10, which says, "Whatever your hand finds to do, do it with all your might." And we also talked about Philippians 2:12 that reads, "Continue to work out your salvation with fear and trembling, for it is God who works in you to will and to act according to his good purpose."

I told him, "Make your wisest choice and trust God to honor it and work through it. You're a godly man. Pray and ask for help, then act boldly." After that, my friend started a home for disadvantaged children and he also became involved in Christian media work. He received no specific guidance to do so – he just did it to honor God. And God has blessed his work.

Divine guidance is not like downloading information from a computer. Decision-making and divine guidance happens in the context of our relationship with God. Our Lord wishes us to trust and rely on him, and also to make wise and godly decisions as his agents on this earth.

18

Temptation and Integrity

A fter reviewing 150 leadership studies, researcher Laura Reave concluded that *personal integrity* is "the most important element for engendering follower respect and trust." [1]

Integrity is one of the most important qualities a missionary can bring to a servant-leadership position. The demonic powers will especially tempt us to compromise our integrity so we will be rendered ineffective. But we need to remember: no one can take our integrity away from us. It is something that we give away ourselves.

Just before Jesus stepped into the national spotlight, Satan tested his integrity in the desert (Matthew 4:1-11). The three trials of integrity he faced are common to all servant-leaders. They are the trials of despair, pride and power.

The First Temptation: Despair

We read how the Spirit of God led Jesus into the desert to hunger. Earlier, when the Israelites hungered in the desert, they despaired and demanded food from God. Jesus just quietly trusted in his Father and affirmed, "Man does not live on bread alone but on every word that comes from the mouth of the Lord" (Deuteronomy 8:3).

In our servant-leadership, there may be times when we are tempted to despair. God may allow us to experience situations that seem beyond our ability to cope. While it is generally unwise for us to work beyond our limits, sometimes we know we must do so to fulfill God's will.

Robert Wilder felt that way in 1886. He was one of a hundred students who sensed the time was ripe to create a student mission movement in America. Wilder was chosen to share this vision in the universities of America, but his health was so precarious that he suffered a total collapse after the first meetings. Risking a permanent breakdown, Wilder decided to continue with his meetings anyways and he trusted God to help him. Over the next eight months, he managed to visit a hundred sixty-two institutions and motivated over two thousand people to serve as missionaries. Almost singlehandedly, he created a student mission movement which became a major factor in bringing the Gospel to Korea, China and India — yet none of it would have happened if Wilder had given up in despair.

Christ maintained his integrity by trusting God for food when others had despaired. Sometimes, we also are called to go beyond our limits in order to do what we know to be right.

The Second Temptation: Pride

In his second attempt to destroy Jesus' integrity as a servant-leader, Satan told Jesus to jump off the Temple in Jerusalem. He even quoted Scripture to ensure his safety. Not even "your foot will suffer harm," he quoted Psalm 91 — as if it were an insurance policy that guaranteed angelic protection.

If Jesus harbored a drop of pride in his heart, he would have jumped. After all, what an amazing miracle it would be! How important Jesus would feel! But Jesus refused to do it because he loved his Father. He would do miracles to fulfill his Father's purposes, but not to make himself feel self-important.

From the desert fathers comes the story of Macarius the Alexandrian, a Desert Father who was a miracle-worker. He was troubled by prideful thoughts that urged him to go to Rome to heal the multitudes there. In the end, however, he chose to remain in the desert because he knew it all came from his pride. [2] Had he gone to heal Rome, he would have lost God. That's why Jesus remained in the desert instead of jumping off the Temple in Jerusalem. And that is why many of the best mission servants just quietly continue to serve in obscure places. To stay true to themselves.

Pride is the desire to be above others so we can have a sense of meaning in our lives. St. John Cassian wrote, "Pride corrupts the whole soul, not just part of it." [3] It does this by deluding us and filling us with a sense of self-importance which makes us incapable of recognizing the value of others. C.S. Lewis wrote in *Mere Christianity* that pride is so individualistic that it "eats up the very possibility of love, or contentment, or even common sense."

Pride is what causes us to listen only to ourselves, or to constantly deride other people, or to conquer others sexually, or to seek an exorbitant salary.

Pride is the chronic sin of the highly-motivated. Charles Colson, who was jailed for the infamous Nixon scandal of the 1970's, spoke repeatedly about the culture of pride that deludes high leaders. Although he once vowed never to be unethical, he admitted in 2008, "I now realize that every human being has an infinite capacity for self-rationalization and self-delusion." In contrast, Jesus says that the kingdom belongs to the "poor in spirit" (Matthew 5:3).

Pride can easily creep into our professionalism. In Paul's day, the Sophists were wandering philosophers who gave public lectures throughout ancient Greece. Impressive in demeanor, looking like erudite professors and employing dazzling rhetorical techniques, the Sophists set the standard of professionalism for the Greek world. Yet, at the heart of Sophic professionalism lay a deep-seated pride. Their focus was all on fame, appearance and acquiring power. In contrast, Paul was not as impressive or as rhetorical as the Sophists, but he had a heart for God and he was authentic (2 Corinthians 10:9-10, 11:6).

Today, it is easy for us to be enamored by a Sophic model of professionalism. We can join in the naked pursuit for power that consumes the lives of so many professionals, or we can realize that our true security lies in God alone. If Jesus had acted like some professionals do today, he would have avoided the Cross at all costs since it was such a horrible career move. Yet, the Cross proved to be the crux of history. There is a difference between power and authority.

Just as pride can affect our professional work, so can humility.

When Boeing designed the 777 jetliner, the company wanted to build the safest plane in the world. To reach that goal, it changed its culture by creating teams committed to working together and reducing error. The previous culture at Boeing was more individualistic in which engineers tried to solve problems on their own to preserve their sense of pride. Now, everyone was forced to be open about the problems they were facing. It was an experiment in organizational humility and it produced a highly successful airliner.

Contrast this with the maiden voyage of the Titanic in 1912. Captain Edward John Smith insisted on racing the vessel at top speed even though icebergs were reported nearby. Foolishly, he wanted to impress the world with the speed of the Titanic's maiden voyage across the icy North Atlantic.

Pride sank the Titanic. Humility helped to create the 777 series of jetliners. Might we say that humility works better?

The Third Temptation: Power

In his third attempt to destroy Jesus' integrity, Satan offered him power. He openly promised him, "Worship me and I'll give you the world!" Well, the world is not his to give, but Satan always seems to convince us otherwise. He tempts us to be ruthless to gain power.

When we serve as missionaries, we will also be tempted to use ruthlessness to gain power.

In his *Gallic Wars*, Julius Caesar boasts how he slaughtered a million Gauls. He never mentions that his campaign was entirely needless and he did it just to win glory for himself. Yet, despite his butchery, Caesar's style was strongly appealing to the Roman world since it epitomized Roman culture. It is not surprising that we find Roman ruthlessness permeating the first churches. Paul writes of evangelists who preached out of "selfish ambition." He also said that, "everyone looks out for his own interests, not those of Jesus Christ." Of Timothy, a true servant-leader, Paul admits, "I have no one else like him" (Philippians 1:17, 2:20-21). It seems that even most of the Christian workers back then had Caesar in their blood.

In the Roman world, pride was a virtue while humility was a derogatory word reserved for slaves. Christ changed that and redefined the meaning of greatness for us. It's down, then up. Serving, then glory. Humility is our virtue, not the arrogant pride of a Caesar. Paul sums up this contrast between Roman and Christian cultures in the hymnic words:

Philippians 2:5-11 *In your relationships with one another, have the same mindset as Christ Jesus: Who, being in very nature God, did not consider equality with God something to be used to his own advantage; rather, he made himself nothing by taking the very nature of a servant, being made in human likeness. And being found in appearance as a man, he humbled himself by becoming obedient to death—even death on a cross! Therefore God exalted him to the highest place and gave him the name that is above every name, that at the name of Jesus every knee should bow, in heaven and on earth and under the earth, and every tongue acknowledge that Jesus Christ is Lord, to the glory of God the Father.*

The narrative of success in so many cultures is the story of the poor person who becomes rich. It is never the rich person who becomes poor. Yet, Jesus said, "whatever you did for one of the least of these brothers and sisters of mine, you did for me" (Matthew 25:40). Henri Nouwen once wrote:

> *The way of the Christian leader is not the way of upward mobility in which our world has invested so much, but the way of downward mobility ending on the cross. Here we touch the most important quality of Christian leadership in the future. It is not a leadership of power and control; but a leadership of powerlessness and humility in which the suffering servant of God, Jesus Christ, is made manifest.* [4]

Even missionaries can be quite ruthless at times. I have witnessed fierce, concealed battles over donors, turf and prestige. Some missionaries are driven to achieve power at any cost, even resorting to slander and defamation to manipulate situations or to preserve their influence. Ruthlessness exists among us, and we must renounce it as the temptation of Satan.

Satan sought to destroy Jesus' ministry by tempting him with despair, pride and power. If Satan had succeeded, Jesus would have lost his integrity. When we serve as missionaries, the demonic will also tempt us to compromise ourselves. The exact trial will be as varied as our human experience, but will usually reflect the same old themes. Satan pokes at our shadow side to make us go berserk with fear and desperation. Jesus handled these temptations by always remembering the sufficiency of his Father's providential care for him.

19

Conflict and Peacemaking

An important skill in mission service is the ability to resolve a conflict. Christians are called to peacemaking since Jesus said, "Blessed are the peacemakers." This is not an option, but an essential part of who we are.

It may be our calling, but conflict is often our companion. Since missionaries are often involved in leadership, our tasks often are to move people toward objectives. We frequently have to deal with intransigent organizational attitudes and competing interests among the people we lead. Sometimes, conflict hardens like concrete in an organization, turning into systemic anger. We may face a whole culture of conflict — marked by hostility, subversion, manipulation, secretiveness and other lingering emotions. All of this can leave us feeling frustrated, annoyed and angry.

Conflict is also a major issue within mission team and is an important reason why many missionaries return to their home countries prematurely. We find it even in the breakup of Paul and Barnabas as a mission team over the matter of John Mark (Acts 15:38-40).

While much is available elsewhere about conflict management, Christian spirituality goes further. It deals with the state of heart that enables us to become peacemakers. Before we can create a culture of peace among the people we serve, we first must understand the anger within our own lives and learn how to deal with it.

Is Anger a Sin?

Many missionaries struggle when they feel angry since Christians have been taught for centuries that anger is a sin. But when we read the Bible we find a more nuanced story.

The most common Hebrew word for anger in the Bible is *aph*. It is used to mean both "nose" and "anger" — because we breathe hard when we get angry! Picture an enraged horse with flared nostrils. The Bible vividly draws upon this image to describe God's anger in 2 Samuel 9, talking about the foundations of the earth being laid bare at the blast from his nostrils. It's God's snorting away in anger.

The Bible is full of similar verses, such as Lamentations 2:3 mentioning the "fierce anger" of God and Jeremiah 7:20 — "My anger ... will be poured out." But such verses make us wonder: if anger is a sin, as we have been told, how could God be angry?

There is also the anger of Jesus to bear in mind. In Mark 3:1-5, Jesus heals a man on the Sabbath, prompting some to condemn him for healing on that day. Mark records how Jesus "looked around at them in anger" for their callousness. In a similar way, in John 2:13-16, Jesus makes a whip and drives out the money changers in high emotion. In Matthew 23, he verbally assails the hypocrisy of the Pharisees. And in Mark 10:13-14, Jesus "was indignant" when his disciples tried to prevent children from coming to him (Mark 10:13-14).

In the Bible, both the God of Israel and Jesus openly display anger. We can only conclude that anger itself is not a sin but an emotion, pure and raw, that comes when something is wrong. That's why the ancient Hebrews could think of God snorting away at evil.

The Bible is an earthy book, but there are always those for whom it seems too emotional. Among the upper classes in ancient Roman society, the philosophy of choice was Stoicism — a reasoned, unemotional way of life. For the Stoics, anger most definitely was a sin, as it was also among the Greek Platonists, who taught that God lacks passion. Both Stoicism and Platonism gave no place for the biblical displays of divine anger.

The Stoic and Platonic bias against anger eventually seeped into Christianity, quietly censoring the biblical portrayals of divine anger in Christian thinking. Despite the Bible's vivid Hebraic descriptions of God's anger, Christian teachers like Augustine and John Cassian taught that God cannot possibly display emotion and that anger is a sin — an idea that continues to the present day.

Yet, despite this, the biblical evidence is plainly there: anger itself is not a sin — it's an emotional response to something that is wrong. The sin lies in the ungodly motives we may have behind our anger and in the destructive behavior which may result from it.

Dealing with Our Anger

When we are angry, the main counsel of the scriptures is to watch our motives and to keep our anger from turning destructive. Although anger is an emotion, it is invariably impure, especially when it is quick anger.

We watch our anger by being emotionally honest with ourselves. Paul writes, "'Be angry, but do not sin': Do not let the sun go down while you are still angry" (Ephesians 4:26). It's only when we are first honest with our anger that we can prevent it from curdling into something sour. Jesus goes so far as to teach that reconciliation is more important than worship itself (Matthew 5:23-24).

We must be especially careful to become angry only for the right reason. In the Bible, God's anger is never vindictive, but always redemptive. Even when God allows the Babylonians to attack Jerusalem, it is to correct its injustice. And when Jesus drives the money changers from the Temple, he is not having a temper-tantrum but purposefully teaching a lesson.

The scriptures counsel us to get angry slowly since this gives us time to reflect and to develop the right motives behind our anger, which often arises from our selfishness, pride, or immaturity. Such anger does not bring about the "righteous life that God desires" (James 1:20, 3:14-16). We read verses such as: "A person with a quick temper does foolish things" (Proverbs 14:17) and "Love ... is not easily angered" (1 Corinthians 13:5). God also is said to be slow to anger (Exodus 34:6).

The cross of Christ also helps us to manage our anger. When we imagine ourselves before the cross and hearing Christ pray for his tormentors, it restrains us. How can we hate a person for whom Christ died, or withhold forgiveness when Jesus prayed for his enemies? Our goal is not to be right; it is to help people to come to God. The cross turns us into peacemakers.

Managing Anger in Others

Once we understand how to deal with our own anger, we become better able to manage it among the people we serve. Our goal is not to suppress anger in others, but to keep it from becoming destructive.

When people are in conflict, they often feel powerless, hopeless, confused, fearful and anxious. An insecure missionary will merely react to these raw emotions and never listen to the real issues. Deep inside, people who are in conflict want to be listened to and respected. They are seeking clear and accurate answers to their questions. Many even wish there could be a win-win outcome and a healing of relationships.

So, our initial goal in a conflict is to move the situation from reaction to conversation. As godly servants, we set the tone by showing respect, making people feel safe and by listening.

Every godly servant should acquire the skill of good listening. When we listen carefully, we are tuning in actively and non-judgmentally to another person. We are allowing others to do the talking. We are showing them genuine interest as we encourage them to express themselves. The psychiatrist and author M. Scott Peck once said, "You cannot truly listen to anyone and do anything else at the same time."

When we listen well, it builds trust and reduces tension and enables people to work together to solve problems. It shifts the focus in the conflict from reacting to responding.

As Christians, prayer also gives us the strength to respond rather than to react. When we are in a conflict, it is easy to regard people as being "trouble-makers" or "obstacles." Jesus commanded us to pray for our enemies because prayer softens our hearts toward our opponents and connects them with us.

Peacemakers and the Beatitudes

The Beatitudes are important for godly servants because they show us how to defuse tense situations. They embody in words what Jesus did on the cross. There, he overcame evil. In the Beatitudes, he teaches us how to transform evil situations.

In the Beatitudes Jesus warned his followers that they would weep and be broken in spirit. They would also be marginalized due to the injustice they would suffer (Matthew 5:3-6). But Jesus also reminded them that they would always have God regardless of what they faced.

I am thinking of an African-American woman in my city. She had a difficult day. At the end of it, she came to a prayer meeting in her church and knelt by her chair to pray. She wept ceaselessly and clutched her chair tightly and would not let go. That day, someone she encountered had shown her blatant prejudice.

"Lord, give me the strength to forgive one more time," she called out over and over, as her brothers and sisters surrounded her in support. She was living in the spirit of the Beatitudes, trying to draw strength from God in an unjust and harsh world.

The first Beatitudes (5:3-6) teach us how to protect ourselves from evil people. The other Beatitudes (5:7-10) show us how to overcome evil itself. We do so by exercising the virtues of mercy, purity and peacemaking:

> *Matthew 5:7-10 Blessed are the merciful, for they will be shown mercy. Blessed are the pure in heart, for they will see God. Blessed are the peacemakers, for they will be called children of God.*

In a conflict, we usually think of ourselves as the victim. But the Beatitudes teach us that we are also to be a responsible party in the reconciliation process. Jesus forces us to stop feeling sorry for ourselves and to start feeling sorry for the perpetrator, who has been caught up by evil. When we do this, it empowers us to conquer evil.

This perspective contrasts markedly with secular thinking, which tends to place all the responsibility for reconciliation on the offending party. But the teaching that the victim should actively work toward reconciliation is also found in the Desert Fathers and the Orthodox Churches. Spiritual formation in the Orthodox tradition includes learning to react to an offense with sympathy and prayer. [1]

The Beatitudes and the Desert Fathers bid us to look within our own hearts when we are in conflict. We cannot bring peace to others unless we first achieve peace within ourselves. Our own pride and anger can exacerbate and prolong a conflict. We have a responsibility to bring healing to our enemies. To make peace break out in an organization, we need to have the heart of a peacemaker. Merely following the techniques of conflict management is not enough. We also need to overcome our own pride and destructive anger and to replace it with the spiritual virtues of humility and compassion and non-judgmentalism.

On Christmas Eve, 1914, a spontaneous peace broke out between opposing forces in World War I. It began when German soldiers in Belgium began singing Christmas carols and English soldiers responded in kind. Soon, opposing soldiers crossed the battlefield and visited one another. Small gifts like whiskey and chocolate were exchanged and there even were sporting matches. After this, the men were reluctant to go back to war, but the enraged politicians and generals forced them to do so. In the ensuing years, commanders even ordered artillery bombings on Christmas Eve to prevent peace from breaking out again. We live in a cruel world, but we can make a difference.

20
Envy and Seeking the Good of Others

One day, I was talking with several students from an urban class I was teaching. Across from me sat Luis, a Latino man in his thirties, and Ephraim, an older African-American leader. Luis couldn't contain his excitement. He said, "I'm learning so much from this class. I'm telling everyone about it!"

It's great having a student like him around.

But then he added, "When I started telling people about what I am learning, they kept on telling me to keep quiet ... they said, 'others have never had the chance to be in school like you.'"

Luis looked puzzled as we all sat there. Then he said, "I still don't understand it. Aren't we supposed to be getting an education and getting ahead?"

That's when Ephraim, older and wiser, spoke. His words were unforgettable: "I've seen this time and again," he intoned. "Whenever someone gets ahead a little, others are not happy about it. Instead, they accuse you of being better than them. Whenever you begin succeeding, there are all these hands trying to pull you back down. But we have to learn to help each other succeed instead."

As we sat there, I realized we were talking about the effects of envy, which makes us jealous over another's success and desirous for their failure instead of their good.

In ancient Greek mythology, as recorded by Ovid, Envy was depicted as a woman holding a handful of snakes and eating them at the same time. She never smiles, except at the sight of someone's troubles. She always frowns at the success of another. She is her own punishment because she is both gnawed within as much as she gnaws at others.

Envy is born out of a lack of contentment with what one has. The Latin for envy is *invidia*, which literally means "not seeing." Dante depicted envious people as walking under cloaks of lead with their eyes sewn shut with wires. They cannot see all that they have from God. Instead, they are filled with feelings of inferiority, resentment and ill-will towards others whom they consider to be more fortunate than themselves.

Similarly, scholars say that Jesus is also referring to envy when he said:

> **Matthew 6:22-23** *If your eyes are healthy, your whole body will be full of light. But if your eyes are unhealthy, your whole body will be full of darkness. If then the light within you is darkness, how great is that darkness!*

Envy is a personal sin with clear, cultural effects. A school teacher, a leader in her own right, once told me, "I have plenty of smart students in my class but teaching them is so frustrating. As soon as my students reach a low-average grade, they stop studying. It's an unwritten rule among them that no one is supposed to get ahead. They're afraid of what the others will say." She was describing the effects of envy within her school's culture.

Envy permeates some cultures to such an extent that special amulets are used in attempts to ward off its effects. Belief in the "evil eye," considered to be an envious look that brings destruction, is common in the Middle East, South Asia, Central Asia, West Africa and Mediterranean Europe. In Islamic cultures, a talisman known as the "hand of Fatima" is used as a gimmick to ward off the evil eye.

Envy and Missionaries

Envy affects missionaries just as much as anyone. If someone advances professionally beyond us, or is more liked personally, or gets chosen to a special assignment, it can make us feel envious. I've had friends who were asked to speak to thousands in international conferences, leaving me wondering, "Humph! Now, how did that happen?"

Envy is the sin of comparison. Every time we think we have not succeeded — failure being whatever we think it is — we envy those who appear to have done better.

Executives often measure their worth by their salary, causing compensations to spiral out of sight. Lee Iacocca, an automotive executive, once admitted, "Sometimes I think the real culprit is envy." The same dynamic is at play among missionaries when we measure our worth by the size of our ministry or our influence among others.

Envy certainly affects the internal interaction of an organization. A successful person on a team, for instance, could evoke others to envy without knowing it. In turn, other team members might then spread gossip to undermine that person. Sometimes we are not even fully aware of our own envy and instead we consign our feelings to the unconscious — creating a culture of hidden subterfuges on a team or in an organization. Self-interest becomes more important than the common good.

The Antidote to Envy

Christian spirituality offers several strategies to cope with envy. The first is to be content with God and what God provides. God loves us. Christ died for us. We are being called to a glorious existence. We have many blessings in our lives. If we open our eyes, we will discover abundant reasons to be content.

From a Christian perspective, we also need to remember that our work is a calling which we receive from God. When we remind ourselves of the nature of our calling from God to be servants, it keeps us from comparing ourselves to others or from turning our work into a competition.

Several of the spiritual disciplines are especially helpful for dealing with envy. Since envy is the failure to seek the good of another, we can personally adopt those spiritual disciplines which best counteract this. One such spiritual discipline is that of mentoring. When we mentor, we selflessly develop the potential of other people. Instead of comparing ourselves with others, we are using our skills and knowledge in a productive way to help others succeed.

Another spiritual discipline that thwarts envy is to be in a covenant group. There, we learn that we are valued as a part of the whole even as we are not the whole. The Spirit bestows on each person a unique spiritual gift which we use for the common good. When we see a friend being used by God, it becomes an occasion to thank God rather than to feel envious. Paul and Peter could have been natural rivals; instead, Scripture tells us that they "recognized the grace" within each other (Galatians 2:7-9).

We also can adopt such a spiritual discipline as deliberately praying for the welfare of those we envy. Or, we can practice the discipline of serving others, such as by volunteering in a project to aid the poor. All of these disciplines help us to overcome envy by seeking the good of others.

21

Bitterness and Forgiveness

Once when I worked as a gardener, I encountered a weed from hell. It was an ordinary-looking plant but as I began tugging at it, I discovered a tap root that raced deep into the soil. Sharp thorns, which easily pierced my thick gloves, covered not only the stalk but the root as well. I dug deeper and deeper and pulled and hacked at it for a whole hour. Once into that fight, I was determined for that blasted root never to grow back.

In the end, the weed won. I yanked out as much as I could without the use of explosives and then simply gave up on a hot summer's day. Yet, I knew the root would reach the surface again. Bitter roots are like that.

In Jesus' time, the root of bitterness ran deep in many hearts. The Roman army had humiliated Judea for decades. Thousands of Jews lost their lives in periodic attempts at freedom. Yet, Jesus told his followers to, "Love your enemies and pray for those who persecute you." He accepted none of his countrymen's reasons to be bitter. He accepts none of ours. We may think we have a right to be bitter or resentful, but Jesus says that it simply is not an option since it can affect our eternal destinies. Instead, we are to overcome bitterness with forgiveness and be like God: "Be perfect, as your heavenly father is perfect," he told us (Matthew 5:48). He also told us to forgive others in our prayers, "if you hold anything against anyone" (Mark 11:25).

Missionaries can always find a reason to become bitter. It may be the people who fail us, or those who talk about us. It may be the unfair scrutiny we receive, or the hard work which goes unnoticed. We can be responsible for many things, yet not have everything under our control. Through the years, resentment can build up like rust in a pipe.

Yet, we are to avoid becoming bitter.

One way is by practicing unconditional forgiveness. This is a spiritual habit of intentionally forgiving others whether or not they admit their fault. The purpose of unconditional forgiveness is to get rid of the toxic waste, whether or not we are proved right. If we wait for people to admit their fault before we forgive them, we're often left to stew in our own juices.

It is to our benefit to forgive unconditionally, since bitter people never amount to much. The opportunities they find never equal their talent, nor do they ever thrive like they should. The reason is simple: no one likes to have vinegary people around. When we choose to forgive, we also are choosing a better future for ourselves.

The Embattled Middle-Manager

Many missionaries find themselves in middle-management positions. They especially have to watch out for bitterness, squeezed as they are between the rank-and-file and senior management. When we field tested this book, a number of missionaries said, "We work under a horrible boss. What can a godly servant do?"

Certainly one thing we can do is to maintain our own spiritual authority. Bad bosses are like terrible tykes — they lack the emotional maturity to handle their feelings of power.

The best way to manage people like that is to be mature ourselves. We are not responsible for the dysfunction of others; we are only responsible for our own mental and spiritual health. This means, when dealing with a difficult boss, we should continue to be open and respectful — being pro-active in solving problems, staying on-task and not allowing an issue to become petty and personal. We can give our positive feedback when management acts in a responsible way. Praying for the leaders we serve under also is very important.

The Anglican *Book of Common Prayer* reminds us: "to honor those in authority and to meet their just demands." In other words, servant-leaders must look beyond their own emotional reactions in situations and focus on being good and wise team players under senior leaders.

The Goal of Forgiveness

The final goal of forgiveness is always full reconciliation.

I once frequented a blighted neighborhood haunted by fire-gutted buildings. After the buildings were razed, every time we passed the empty lots we continued to remember those buildings. In time, however, a new neighborhood was created when beautiful townhouses were built where the old buildings had been and families moved in and filled the streets with salsa music. It was only after the new neighborhood was built that we finally forgot about the rotted buildings.

The process of reconciliation is like that. Some people never tear down their bitter buildings. They see them every day as they pass by. Others level their buildings, but then they see empty lots for the rest of their lives. Only some of us create a new neighborhood and experience true healing.

The ultimate goal of forgiveness is reconciliation — healing the past by finding a future. This can be a messy process. People may have to experience consequences for their actions, even legal consequences, before they will change. But always the goal is the same: to forget the old neighborhood in order to live in the new.

Organizational Forgiveness

Forgiveness is not just for individuals. It can also be practiced in organizations.

When an organization practices forgiveness, the people within it choose together to leave behind their resentment and grudges over a perceived harm and they work toward a new future. Forgiveness characterizes healthy organizations.

Organizational forgiveness is not an attempt to minimize harm. Instead, it is a response to keep that perceived harm from becoming part of the organization's culture. It ends internal dysfunctions by healing bitterness, making peace and creating a positive outcome. It frees people so they can move forward optimistically.

It is important to promote organizational forgiveness when we serve in a stressed organization, such as during times of downsizing. Almost always, such organizations fall into conflict, resentment, blame and scapegoating. Attitudes turn rigid, preventing the organization from finding the resiliency it needs to create a new future. To break the downward cycle, people must forgive the harm.

In one hospital I served, a budget crisis threatened jobs. The executive leadership made an extraordinary effort to reduce costs to avoid firing as few people as possible. They were honest about the problem and made personal sacrifices themselves. In the end, the staff avoided turning bitter and even were deeply appreciative of what was being done for them. They willingly made their own sacrifices to help.

On the other hand, I served another organization which had been under stress due to a series of leadership scandals. The people in it were divided and bitter, so my leadership in that institution became a matter of helping people to get over their past. In a series of dicey meetings, we worked through the bitterness and helped people to develop positive attitudes.

One of the most noted examples of organizational forgiveness in history occurred in South Africa after apartheid ended in 1990. For fifty years, the apartheid regime had kept the races apart. Terrible, gruesome killings happened and the minority whites adopted a dehumanizing attitude toward the majority black citizens. Atrocities, such as the Sharpeville massacre of 1960, embittered many. When apartheid ended and the majority races came to power, a bloodbath was expected.

Yet, the national leadership at that time, which included Nelson Mandela and Bishop Desmond Tutu, exemplified forgiveness. Upon his election as president of South Africa, Mandela established the Truth and Reconciliation Commission, chaired by Bishop Tutu. It granted complete amnesty to all apartheid-motivated crimes — including torture, murder and rape — provided that the confessor spoke publicly and voluntarily, telling the whole truth and acknowledging the wrong which had been done.

The Commission helped to create a new South Africa. Bishop Tutu remarked, "As I listened to the stories of victims I marveled at their magnanimity, that after so much suffering, instead of lusting for revenge, they had this extraordinary willingness to forgive."

When we are harmed, we feel we have a right to be bitter and usually forgiveness is the last thing on our minds. Yet, bitterness makes us unhappy and, eventually, we just get sick of it all. The way back to happiness, Jesus teaches, is by forgiving. Forgiveness can be difficult, since it runs contrary to our emotions. Yet, once we do it, it frees us from the harm that happened. Evil does not have to affect our lives forever. We can find love and God again.

Postscript:
A Word to Mission Executives

I f you are a mission executive, you may be wondering what is the best way to promote spiritual formation within your organization. Below, I offer a few basic suggestions.

1. State It in Your Five-year Goals

First, it would be important to incorporate intentional spiritual formation into your five-year organizational goals. So often, we just leave spiritual formation up to the individual. What we are talking about is something quite different. Organizations can purposefully choose to deepen their own spirituality, but it requires time, effort and commitment.

In thinking through this matter, your governing board may wish to consider the following questions:

How has the spiritual health of our organization changed over time?

Are we making decisions today in a godly way?

Has secularism begun to affect the way we do things?

Are we giving adequate place to the Spirit?

Are we truly relying on prayer and providence?

Do we give meaningful time to worship?

Do our members have an adequate theology of spiritual formation?

2. Form a Cadre

The people who will best promote intentional spiritual formation within an organization will be those for whom it is their vision and passion. Right now, God may be raising up these individuals in your midst. I encourage you to do what it takes to train these people until they become your spiritual formation cadre.

It is best for their training to be done in evangelical organizations. In the past, some evangelicals received their training through Catholic channels because so little was available from evangelical institutions.

As helpful as this training from Catholic channels has been, we should realize that there are theological emphases in the Roman Catholic spiritual formation tradition which are not shared in classic Protestantism. We have tried to explain some of these differences in this book, such as the Catholic idea that spiritual formation is a progression rather than a maturation, or that the contemplative lifestyle is superior to working in the world. When spiritual formation missionaries begin thinking like this, it can alienate them from their fellow evangelical missionaries unless the concepts are carefully re-thought to be communicable to evangelicals. If this is not done well, the result can lead to needless misunderstanding and tension. So, it is essential for your cadre not only to receive academic training which helps them to understand the breadth of Christian spirituality through the centuries, but which is also consistent with evangelical thinking.

Fortunately, there are now an increasing number of evangelical programs available for spiritual formation. Since these change over time, I suggest that you contact spiritual formation professors from evangelical seminaries for specific suggestions.

3.   Train Your Mission Teams

Once your cadre is formed and adequately trained, empower them to become your change agents within your organization. This is best done as a gradual process with abundant feedback, guidance and mid-course corrections.

It may be best for your cadre to first develop a spiritual formation training program for your organization and then present it gradually to your teams. You might also consider the use of retreat centers and retreat leaders as part of your continuing program. Some missions now require their partners to go on a personal spiritual retreat at least once a year.

It is especially important that you and your cadre address any issues of isolation that may exist among your individual missionaries. Spiritual formation happens best in authentic communities where there is openness, trust and accountability. How might such communities be fostered in your mission?

Finally, we hope that our website, www.godlyservants.org, will be available for a number of years to provide additional resources for you and your organization.

Reading Suggestions

Hundreds of books are now available concerning discipleship and spiritual formation. Below is my short list of quality books that would be a good place for anyone to begin:

Andrews, Alan, ed., *The Kingdom Life: A Practical Theology of Discipleship and Spiritual Formation.*

Calhoun, Adele Ahlberg, *Spiritual Disciplines Handbook.*

Chan, Simon, *Spiritual Theology: A Systematic Study of the Christian Life.*

Foster, Richard J., *Streams of Living Water.*

Foster, Richard J., *Celebration of Discipline.*

Foyle, Marjory F., *Honourably Wounded: Stress among Christian Workers.*

Johnson, Reginald, *Your Personality and the Spiritual Life.*

Lovelace, Richard, *Dynamics of Spiritual Life: An Evangelical Theology of Renewal.*

Nouwen, Henri, *The Wounded Healer.*

McIntosh, Gary L. and Samuel D. Rima, Sr., *Overcoming the Dark Side of Leadership: The Paradox of Personal Dysfunction.*

Palmer, G. E. H., Philip Sherrard and Kallistos Ware, trans. and eds. *The Philokalia.*

Pettit, Paul, ed., *Foundations of Spiritual Formation: A Community Approach to Becoming Like Christ.*

Stott, John R. W., *The Cross of Christ.*

Vanier, Jean, *From Brokenness to Community.*

Notes

Chapter Two: The Soul of a Servant
1. http://vimeo.com/6085134
2. Joris Lammers et al., "Power Increases Hypocrisy: Moralizing in Reasoning, Immorality in Behavior" in *Psychological Science* (2010), pp. 737-744.

Chapter Three: Becoming Sensitive to God
1. The Desert Fathers developed a list of the most powerful sins common to the human condition. St. John Cassian obtained the list and promoted it in the Western Roman Empire through his *Institutes* and *Conferences* (written around 425-428 AD). The original list consisted of eight items. Today, it has been reworked into the "Seven Deadly Sins": pride, envy, gluttony, lust, anger, greed and sloth.
2. Augustine, *Confessions* 8.12.
3. *Confessions* 10.3.
4. *On Guarding the Intellect*, 17.

Chapter Four: Going Deeper with God
1. *Spiritual Exercises*, section 336.

Chapter Five: Contemplative Prayer
1. *Catechism of the Catholic Church*, 2709.
2. Thomas Dubay, *Fire Within* (1989), chapter 5.

Chapter Seven: Spiritual Disciplines
1. See, for instance, Reginald Johnson, *Your Personality and the Spiritual Life* (1999). In a similar way, Adele Ahlberg Calhoun in *Spiritual Disciplines Handbook* (2005) also defines

which spiritual disciplines are most appropriate for the varying seasons of life.
2. Another name for the Story of God is the "biblical metanarrative." For more, see my article at http://www.postmodernpreaching.net/metanarrative.htm

Chapter Eight: A Life Review Retreat
1. John Calvin, *Institutes of the Christian Religion*, 1:35,37.
2. I first encountered this style of retreat at a seminar led by Dr. Tom Ashbrook. The following is an adaptation.

Chapter Nine: Spiritual Warfare
1. For a description of the stages of yielding to a temptation, see G. E. H. Palmer, Philip Sherrard and Kalistos Ware (eds.), *The Philokalia* Vol. 1 (London, 1979), pp. 365-367.
2. For more on discernment, see pp. 98-108 in *The Philokalia* Vol. 1 (1979).

Chapter Ten: Community and Spiritual Formation
1. Quoted in Paul Pettit, ed. *Foundations of Spiritual Formation: A Community Approach to Becoming Like Christ* (2008), pp. 10, 13.
2. News release from Rush University Medical Center, 23 February 2010.

Chapter Twelve: Respecting the Spirituality of Others
1. There are a number of books available which can help you explore the interrelationship between personality and spirituality, but I especially recommend Reginald Johnson's *Your Personality and the Spiritual Life* (1999).

Chapter Thirteen: Solitude
1. Henri J. M. Nouwen, *Making All Things New* (1981), p. 69.

2. Richard J. Foster, *Prayer: Finding the Heart's True Home* (1992), pp. 63, 100.
3. Thomas Merton, *The Sign of Jonas* (1953), pp. 91-92.
4. Marjory F. Foyle, *Honourably Wounded: Stress among Christian Workers* (1987), p. 32.

Chapter Fourteen: Leading in Community

1. Laura Reave, "Spiritual Values & Practices Related to Leadership Effectiveness," *The Leadership Quarterly* (2005, pp. 655-687).
2. *On Discrimination*, 13.
3. J. Oswald Sanders, *Spiritual Leadership* (1967), page 107.

Chapter Seventeen: Decision-Making and Guidance

1. Simon Chan, *Spiritual Theology: A Systematic Study of the Christian Life* (1998), pp. 151-152.

Chapter Eighteen: Temptation and Integrity

1. Laura Reave, "Spiritual Values & Practices Related to Leadership Effectiveness," *The Leadership Quarterly* (2005, pp. 655-687).
2. The story is found in *The Paradise of the Holy Fathers*, book 1, chapter 18. The *Paradise* preserves stories of the Desert Fathers from the period 250-400 AD.
3. St. John Cassian, *On the Eight Vices: On Pride*.
4. Henri Nouwen, *In the Name of Jesus: Reflections on Christian Leadership* (1996), pp. 62-63.

Chapter Nineteen: Conflict and Peacemaking

1. Elizabeth A. Gassin, "Interpersonal Forgiveness from an Eastern Orthodox Perspective," *Journal of Psychology and Theology,* (2001).